It All Happened in

Renfro Valley

It All Happened in

Renfro Valley

PETE STAMPER

THE UNIVERSITY PRESS OF KENTUCKY

Publication of this volume was made possible in part
by a grant from the National Endowment for the Humanities.

Scholarly publisher for the Commonwealth,
serving Bellarmine University, Berea College, Centre
College of Kentucky, Eastern Kentucky University,
The Filson Historical Society, Georgetown College,
Kentucky Historical Society, Kentucky State University,
Morehead State University, Murray State University,
Northern Kentucky University, Transylvania University,
University of Kentucky, University of Louisville,
and Western Kentucky University.
All rights reserved.

Editorial and Sales Offices: The University Press of Kentucky
663 South Limestone Street, Lexington, Kentucky 40508-4008
www.kentuckypress.com

12 11 10 09 08   6 5 4 3 2

Library of Congress Cataloging-in-Publication Data

Stamper, Pete, 1930–
    It all happened in Renfro Valley / by Pete Stamper
        p.   cm.
    Includes index.
    ISBN-10: 0-8131-2140-X (alk. paper).
    ISBN-10: 0-8131-0975-2 (pbk: alk. paper)
    1. Country music—Kentucky—Renfro Valley—History and criticism.
2. Renfro Valley Barn Dance (Radio program)—History. 3. Lair, John
4. Renfro Valley (Ky.)—Social life and customs. I. Title.
ML 3524.S73   1999
781.642'09769'623—dc21   99-29031
ISBN-13: 978-0-8131-0975-6 (pbk. : alk. paper)

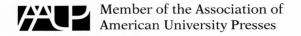 Member of the Association of
American University Presses

To John, Kirbit, and Gefus, my three imaginary playmates who shared my childhood days in rural Butler county. Clarence Williams, James Milton, and Clifton Sisk, real honest-to-goodness pals who ran beside me all the way to manhood. To John Lair, Red Foley, and Don Warden who gave a young entertainer all the help he could use. To Glenn Pennington, Ralph Gabbard, and Warren Rosenthal for the icing on my cake, a layer higher than I ever thought it would be.

Just a little over a year ago when I set out on this journey "back down this road a piece," I became aware of just how many of the players who had had a part in Renfro Valley's early years had made their final curtain call. I remember counting my blessings there was still one I could count on to either confirm or reject my memory on a number of events.

Old Joe Clark who had celebrated his 50th anniversary in the Renfro Valley spotlight not only remembered how and why this or that took place the way it did, he was the whole story on many occasions in what I have to say.

Old Joe was just two weeks away from beginning his 52nd season when he took his final bow on the stage of life. I have left each story about my friend as it was originally written and approved by him and in the present tense since he is in our minds at each time we step on stage. I am proud to say they brought him a chuckle or two.

Thanks, Joe, for the memories.

Contents

A Note from Dolly Parton

Pete Stamper is to me and many others one of the funniest and most original comedians ever in our business. I love his delivery; he kinda sneaks up on you. His humor is smart and funny, and that's a great combination. Pete is not only unique as a comedian but as a human being as well. I traveled with Pete long enough to pick him apart if there had been anything to pick at. I think he is a perfect gentleman—respectful, reserved, quiet—and you would think he is anything but a comedian except for his funny twist on everything. He reminds me a great deal of Will Rogers. I love him.

Renfro Valley has meant so much to every person in country music, especially older folks like me. We have all played there or played with people who have, and we think of it as legend.

Dolly

Foreword

Wayne W. Daniel

Renfro Valley, Kentucky, is located in Rockcastle County on the edge of the Daniel Boone National Forest, near the intersection of Interstate 75 and U.S. 25. It is sixty miles south of Lexington, Kentucky, and 120 miles north of Knoxville, Tennessee. At first, Renfro was merely the name of a creek that trickled through the forests and meadows near Mt. Vernon, Kentucky, and was known only to the few mountain folks who called the area home. Today, Renfro Valley is an entertainment complex whose nucleus is country music in all its various forms and related genres. As a mecca for fans of country music, it rivals Branson, Missouri, and Nashville's Grand Ole Opry. From a 1930s Saturday night combination radio broadcast and stage show, the musical menu at Renfro Valley has evolved into a smorgasbord of shows and mini-concerts featuring old-time country music, country gospel, modern country, bluegrass, and country comedy. Headliner concerts featuring Nashville's top country artists and special events such as fiddler's festivals and all-night gospel sings supplement the roster of regular Renfro Valley entertainers and scheduled events. Between shows, visitors pass the time strolling the streets of a Victorian-style village featuring craft shops and restaurants, visiting a log schoolhouse, resting body and soul in a little country church, or learning about the history of Renfro Valley at the village museum.

The originator of the Renfro Valley entertainment center was the valley's most widely known native son, John Lair. Born July 1, 1894, in Rockcastle County, Lair grew up in the community that he later named. The culture that helped shape the young Lair included a mixture of both sacred and secular components. On Sundays there were church services to attend where the congregation sang hymns and songs of a serious nature, a community leader imparted words of wisdom and advice to the young folks, and a circuit-riding preacher occasionally dropped by to treat the worshipers to a real sermon. During the week, entertainment was to be found at such community functions as play-parties, square dances, pie suppers, and singing bees. John Lair absorbed his culture like a sponge, and as an adult he drew on his store of youthful impressions to build one of the country's greatest monuments to nostalgia, Renfro Valley.

Lair was deeply interested in music, especially the music that had been created or appropriated by the masses and handed down from generation to generation. Ancient ballads such as "Barbara Allen" and "The Gypsy's Warning" as well as traditional fiddle tunes such as "Soldier's Joy" and "Devil's Dream" held as much interest for him as spinning wheels, flintlock rifles, and other physical artifacts with stories to tell of America's olden days.

In the thirties, Lair worked with a radio program, the *National Barn Dance*, on Chicago's WLS. In Burridge D. Butler, owner of WLS, Lair found a sympathetic and kindred soul.[1] Butler, like Lair, was fascinated with the past, was a champion of the farmer and the agrarian way of life, and was constantly promoting traditional family values among those who worked for him, those who listened to his radio station, and those who read his newspaper.[2] One of the first things Lair did was go back home to Renfro Valley and round up local talent that he put on the air as performers on the *National Barn Dance* and other WLS programs. Using a programming format that would become his trademark, he presented these singers and musicians to their radio audiences in mountaineer sketches, which, as station officials once noted, "touched so many hearts."[3]

Though the *WLS National Barn Dance* was designed to *simulate* an old-fashioned rural hoe-down, Lair wanted to give radio listeners *the real thing*. His dream was to be able to broadcast a barn dance from a real barn using local musicians, and he wanted that barn to be in Renfro Valley. The next step along the way came in 1937 when he acquired a sponsor willing to pay for a Saturday night radio show called the *Renfro Valley Barn Dance*. The show premiered on October 9, 1937, and was staged at the Cincinnati Music Hall and broadcast over WLW. It included crooner Red Foley; fiddler/comedian Slim Miller; Millie and Dolly Good, known as the Girls of the

Golden West; Lily May Ledford and the Coon Creek Girls; and the comedy team of A'nt Idy and Little Clifford.[4]

Lair was a dreamer, a historian, a philosopher, and a reveler in the past. But he was stuck with the twentieth century. Realizing that he could not reverse the forward movement of time, he set about the task of staying its course. After years of dreaming, planning, and scheming, his labors bore fruit, and his anachronistic Renfro Valley was finally built in Rockcastle County in 1939. It became known as "the valley where time stands still."

On November 4, 1939, radio listeners across the country who were tuned to Cincinnati's WLW heard the announcer say, "Friends, the long-awaited moment has arrived, and we are now about to take you down to Renfro Valley. . . . Since three o'clock this afternoon the hill folks have been coming on foot, on horseback, and in big farm wagons. At least three hayride parties are reported on the way and reservations have been made from five states, so plenty of strangers and 'furriners' will be on hand for the opening tonight. And now it's time to join them."[5] Following the theme song, "We're Gonna Have a Big Time Tonight," John Lair took over the microphone, greeting listeners with "Howdy, folks! Welcome to the *Renfro Valley Barn Dance* coming to you direct from a big barn in Renfro Valley, Kentucky—the first and only barn dance on the air presented by the actual residents of an actual community."[6]

In his search for talent, Lair's greatest discovery was probably Red Foley, who later became a country music superstar. Other young men and women from Kentucky entered the country music field at about the same time that Foley joined the WLS roster of entertainers. Unlike Foley, for the most part their fame was short-lived and geographically limited. Lair, no doubt, deserves considerable credit for Foley's success. For, although Lair had great respect for the raw talent he uncovered in the hills and hollows of the South, he knew what had to be done to make this talent palatable. He knew just how much polish it took to turn a real mountaineer into an accomplished performer without destroying his or her rustic appeal.

Lair was a stickler for authenticity. To add further to his program's real-life ambiance he convinced station management to allow him to broadcast the shows before live audiences. When Lair's performers took the stage in Renfro Valley, their costumes reflected the dress of the rural southern mountaineer. In 1940 Lair hired a male trio called the Range Riders, who had been singing western songs and dressing in cowboy outfits. Before he let them go on stage at Renfro Valley, he changed their name to the Mountain Rangers, dressed them in plaid shirts, gabardine trousers, and flat-heeled boots, and required them to develop a repertoire of old-time southern hill country songs. "There are no cowboys in Renfro Valley," he said, and for years, during a time when western music was highly popular in movies, on juke boxes, and on the radio, none of his performers were allowed to invoke the cowboy or cowgirl image.[7]

Lair periodically took to the hinterlands of the South in search of folk ballads, play-party songs, and fiddle tunes indigenous to the region. He questioned old-timers about the history and sources of the songs that he would take back for his performers to sing on his radio programs. He attended folk festivals and established professional relationships with folk song scholars and promoters such as George Pullen Jackson and Bascome Lamar Lunsford.[8]

Lair not only collected folk songs; he also sought out old sheet music and song books, sources of long forgotten compositions that found new life on his programs. Among his sources of published music were WLS and *Prairie Farmer* listeners and readers, who responded generously to his pleas for old songs.[9] By mid-1935, thanks in large measure to Lair's efforts, the WLS music library boasted holdings of more than twelve thousand pieces of printed music.[10]

Thus it was that John Lair established for himself a reputation as a man who could turn talented mountaineers into accomplished radio artists and a man who had a vast knowledge and understanding of folk music and folklore of the South. When potential sponsors wanted to put their money behind a rural-oriented radio program that had the ring of authenticity, Lair was the man to see. His Saturday night barn dances, community play-parties, and Sunday morning gatherings were heard across the country on network radio. His approach to radio programming was copied by other broadcast entrepreneurs, and aspiring artists of the airwaves far from the hills of Kentucky sang the songs that he had rescued from oblivion.

In 1940, Ralph W. Griffin described the new barn and a typical Saturday night at Renfro Valley. He wrote:

> Except for its size the barn is just about what one would expect to see upon any reasonably prosperous farm. Inside it is floored, equipped with its capacity of ordinary collapsible seats and a peanut roost, while across the front end there is a large and well-

lighted stage. The lighting effects come from unique electric lanterns and orthodox foot-lights. Ears of corn are strung upon the walls and baled hay is piled about helter-skelter, among pieces of harness and farm machinery. The performers come and go at will. They sit or lounge about upon the bales of hay and upon the floor. Quite often they are to be seen down in the audience, chatting with friends. There is much ad-libbing and impromptu clowning, not to mention a lot of good-natured horseplay. There is no curtain across the front of the stage and once the show starts it is practically continuous. It opens . . . with a thirty-minute broadcast, the program for which is prearranged, well executed and the technique of which is familiar to most radio listeners. One may wander about the parking lot which surrounds the barn and there see car license plates representing possibly fifteen different states, and just any number of Kentucky counties. Swanky limousines may be seen parked alongside ancient farm trucks [and] large busses vie with farm wagons for favorable parking space. Inside the barn, overalls are seated alongside expensive tailored suits, while gingham dresses rub shoulders with Paris gowns.[11]

When listeners to the *Barn Dance* radio broadcasts were invited to write in for a free picture of the cast, the station received fifty-three thousand requests within the next four days. The number of requests eventually reached 253,000. On some Saturday nights more than ten thousand people sought admission to the barn, and frequently it was necessary to keep the show going all night long to accommodate all who had bought tickets.[12] Noting the popularity of the barn dance, the Columbia Broadcasting System (CBS), through the facilities of WHAS in Louisville, picked up the broadcast for airing over its network of radio stations. Other radio programs from Renfro Valley followed.

With the coming of television, the *Renfro Valley Barn Dance* broadcasts, like most live radio shows, were canceled. But people kept coming to Renfro Valley, and to the present day the show has continued to provide visitors with entertainment as a stage production. The one Renfro Valley program that remained on radio was the *Renfro Valley Gatherin'*. This weekly show, performed before a Sunday morning audience at Renfro Valley, is taped for distribution to a syndicate of more than 160 radio stations serving an area from New York to Wyoming and from Wisconsin to Florida.[13]

During most of its first fifty years of existence, the *Renfro Valley Barn Dance* and related enterprises were owned and operated by John Lair or his descendants. Following Lair's death in 1985, the Renfro

Valley entertainment complex was sold, and its current owner is Lexington, Kentucky, businessman, Warren W. Rosenthal.

What one finds at Renfro Valley today is a tasteful blend of the old and new, both in physical structures and entertainment fare. Alongside the original barn is a new auditorium equipped with state-of-the-art seating and audio and video capabilities. On the stage of the old barn, bales of hay have been replaced by a drum stand and amplifiers for electrified instruments. The current slate of entertainers on the *Renfro Valley Barn Dance, Sunday Morning Gatherin',* and the Valley's other shows represents a wide variety of stylists ranging from comedians to gospel quartets. Typical shows feature old-time parlor ballads, novelty songs, bluegrass tunes, and country fare, both classic and modern. The latest hits from Nashville's hottest songwriters are intermingled with songs that John Lair, decades ago, brought back from his trips to the surrounding countryside or culled from stacks of ancient sheet music.

So there you have a gist of the *substance* of Renfro Valley—its origin, a glimpse of its history, its physical features, and some of the human activity that animates it. In the pages that follow, long-time Renfro Valley entertainer Pete Stamper acquaints you with the *soul* of Renfro Valley. Through his warm and often humorous behind-the-scenes anecdotes and human interest stories about the entertainers, you will gain rare insight into the workings of one of America's oldest country music entertainment venues.

References

1. Ann Lair Henderson, *On The Air . . . with John Lair* (Polly House Publications, Mt. Vernon, Kentucky, 1998), p. 6.

2. James F. Evans, *Prairie Farmer and WLS: The Burridge D. Butler Years* (University of Illinois Press, Urbana, 1969), *passim.*

3. *Behind the Scenes at WLS* (Prairie Farmer Publishing Company, Chicago, 1932), p. 11.

4. *Renfro Valley Keepsake,* 1940, unpaginated.

5. "Musical Heritage of Renfro Valley," undated one-page typescript. Courtesy Mrs. Ann Lair Henderson.

6. Ibid.

7. Personal communication with Mrs. Ann Lair Henderson, November 23, 1998.

8. *Standby,* September 14, 1935, p. 3 and July 20, 1935, p. 12; *Renfro Valley Bugle,* April 1947, p. 1.

9. *Standby,* October 5, 1935, p. 12.

10. Ibid., August 17, 1935, p. 11.

11. Ralph W. Griffin, *So This is Renfro Valley: A Brief History* (Mt. Vernon, Kentucky, 1940), unpaginated.

12. *Renfro Valley Keepsake,* 1947, p. 33.

13. *Renfro Valley Bugle,* September 1998, p. 24.

Preface

A number of times during the past five or six years friends of mine have said to me, "You know, you should write a book about Renfro Valley." Not once do I remember ever saying I wouldn't know where to start because I always thought that the start would be the easiest part of all. You can't spend forty-seven years in a place like Renfro Valley without hearing or reading about its beginning a few hundred times. I've searched my mind to recall every corner, nook, and cranny of this little old valley that holds a memory or two or three or four or more for me . . . the swimmin' hole in Renfro Creek where I once frolicked with the Callaway sisters; the two-story log cabin where I got my first and almost my last taste of moonshine; the hamburger steak dinners I ate daily at the Renfro Valley Lodge; the ghostly footsteps that haunt the Museum Building; the peck, peck, pecking sounds from the typewriter coming from inside Mr. Lair's office; the National Anthem playing over the speaker in the breezeway of the radio station as WRVK left the air at sundown; the sounds of the frogs along Renfro Creek where I once frolicked with the Callaway sisters; the chirpin' of the baby birds in the Old Barn loft as we recorded The *Sunday Morning Gatherin'*; the ring of Emory Martin's five-string banjo on a Saturday night as he picked, "Bill Bailey Won't You Please Come Home"; the burst of laughter Slim Miller brought on when he would show off his new shoes; the good feeling I get when I hear someone I have never met call my name as I walk down the Village street; a wave from Dan, Dan the Candyman on my early morning trips to the post office in Renfro Village; the Valley Drive-In where we went to watch

Old Joe Clark in his first moving picture show; of having Mr. Lair find the wet tracks of the Volkswagen I drove through the breezeway of the Museum Building the night before; of hearing my voice as I tell him, "I think Vester Parker owns a car like that"; getting thrown in the annual donkey ball game at the horse show grounds; having coffee with my date around the curve at Belly Acres Restaurant; the sight of the annual flash flood down Renfro Creek where I once frolicked with the Callaway sisters; the night Roy Starkey was rushed from the *Barn Dance* stage to the hospital following a heart attack; hearing Doc Lewis later say, "I'm sorry we lost your buddy last night"; seeing my first Hollywood movie stars when they appeared in person in the Old Barn for the premier of *It Happens Every Thursday;* Red Foley's surprise visit to the *Barn Dance* catching me on stage impersonating Red Foley; seeing the American flag flying above the old post office from one of the center poles from the old show tents; receiving the first annual Lifetime Achievement Award from Warren Rosenthal; receiving the last annual Boo Boo Award from Warren Rosenthal; placing articles in the time capsule at the foot of the stage in the New Barn; the click, click, clicking sound of Virginia Sutton's high-heeled shoes as she crossed the floor of the breezeway from the radio station office to the control room many times a day; the pond with fish in it too old and wise to catch; the fish I used to catch up and down Renfro Creek where I once . . . caught so many I couldn't carry them home—so many memories of my life and times at Renfro Valley.

1930 to 1950

The Early Years of John Lair

On November 4, 1939, the doors of the Old Barn opened on the very first performance of the *Renfro Valley Barn Dance* from Renfro Valley. But that is not where we start. The Renfro Valley Folks were organized in Cincinnati two years prior to this big grand opening. But even that's not the beginning.

To tell the Renfro Valley story we have to go way back, back to 1894. On July 1st of that year the second child and only son of Isabelle Coffey and Thomas Bert Lair was born and named for all his childless uncles, John Allen Leander Jones Porter Armestead Adams Lair. This was according to information given me in 1975 when I was chosen to emcee a program honoring the life of this man. The family Bible, my script went on to say, shortened that name to John Lee Lair. John's sister, Virginia Clyde, was five when he was born, not in Renfro Valley, I must add, but ten miles south in Livingston, Kentucky. His folks had lived in Renfro Valley but, for a reason I never learned, moved away and then returned when young John was five. Mr. Lair has always jokingly said that they moved just to prevent him from being born in Renfro Valley. But at the age of five, John Lair started life on a farm back in Renfro Valley and we have every reason to believe that he enjoyed that life to the fullest. I must admit I have trouble picturing John Lair down on the farm, other than maybe in his childhood. I'm sure that's because I've known him only in a role far removed from tilling the soil. A gentleman farmer, maybe, but never following the plow.

Somewhere early on in this young man's life, something or someone sparked an interest in the past—a spark that grew into an obsession with the history pertaining to a wide range of people, places and things, but mostly around the lives of those who settled the land that he called home. He marveled at the pioneer spirit and reached into their lives and sought out the tender places in the hearts of these rough individuals. This interest never left him and became a part of everything that he accomplished. Over his lifetime he accumulated a library of sheet music that was considered to be one of the best and largest private collections. I found most interesting the information he had in his memory of many of the authors and the stories behind the stories told in the songs.

His knowledge of Abraham Lincoln went much beyond just the songs Lincoln loved. I've heard him discuss Lincoln's sense of humor, wit and wisdom and speculate on the connection between Lincoln's fits of depression and a kick in the head by a mule he experienced when he was a boy. He retraced the steps of Daniel Boone and his party and, of course, those of James, John, and Lula Renfro into the wilderness of Kentucky. He tracked at least one Kentuckian from Rockcastle County to the Alamo where he fought alongside Crockett and Bowie. He was fascinated with the lives of some of the bad men of the West, especially those of Jesse James and his brother Frank. He knew the true story of that famous railroad engineer, and he got that story direct from his widow, Mrs. Casey Jones. And his stories of the Civil War and mountain feuds could keep you spellbound for hours. No, John Lair wasn't a man of the soil, but there is no doubt he was a student of history.

John Lair began his education in the little log Redbud Schoolhouse that stood up the creek about four miles, the same little Redbud Schoolhouse where his father had gone to school, the same Redbud Schoolhouse that now stands in Renfro Village. When it came time for his high school education, he had to travel to the county seat, Mt. Vernon, and was one of the three members to graduate from the new high school in 1914. After twenty years of his life had passed he left Renfro Valley for the very first time with more than his share of ambition and enough of the old pioneer spirit he admired so much in others to take him into uncharted waters on more than one occasion.

John Lair was a master storyteller although only fair when it came to telling a joke, mainly because his story was embellished to the point that it overshadowed the punch line. However, his sense of humor was one of the finest I've ever seen. It didn't surprise me to

(*Left*) John Lair
(*Below*) The Old Barn, circa 1944

learn that his journey out into the world was to enroll in a cartoonist school that took young John up north, many miles from home. Now, I'm no judge of cartoons, but those I've seen that he did a little later in life looked like they could have compared fairly with the best of them. I think most would agree that John was a home boy and I would suspect his short stay in that school was more because of homesickness than anything else.

When he returned home he made use of the education that he had and tried to pass some of it on to others. He taught school in Livingston for a while and in Mt. Vernon. One of the pupils in his Mt. Vernon class would one day become Mrs. John Lair.

In just two years after graduating from high school and before he could get established in his new profession, he was drafted into the army during World War I. The army assigned him to special services and stationed him at Camp Meigs in Washington, D.C. I've heard tell by those who knew him when he was growing up that he always managed to be the center of attention, but that love of the spotlight may have grown a little stronger during his tour with Uncle Sam. His special service unit teamed with Ziegfeld to do an army review show in Washington called *Atta Boy*, for which he wrote several sketches.

I'm told that in the spring of 1918, Helen Ware, a famous actress of the day, was appearing at the National Theatre in Washington. John was invited to attend and was surprised with a special seat in the box alongside his commanding general. During her performance Miss Ware recited a poem entitled "Before I Crossed," written by Mr. Lair, and then announced that the author was in the audience. She walked to the side of the stage and invited John into the spotlight. I wonder if this could be when the show biz bug got its first nibble at John Lair.

The cartoons that I have seen were those that he drew for a book of poems that he wrote while in the army titled *Lest We Forget*. All this special attention earned him a furlough and it came just at the right time, for while he was home his father died. Young John was allowed to leave the army as he was the sole support of his mother. It was during this time on the farm at about the age of twenty-four or twenty-five that he first began to have a dream of a Renfro Valley that would be as special to future generations as it had been to him. He said, and I quote, "In the early twilight of long summer days I often sat on a big rock topping the highest hill back of the home place and dreamed foolish dreams that sometime or another come to all boys. Impossible dreams, maybe, but the kind that are hard to get rid of. I thought what I would do if I had money enough to own the whole valley some-day. My dream was not one of conquest and advancement such as had led the early settlers in Renfro Valley to work hard, to build up a settlement, and dream of progress and growth. My dream was in a way to move backward across the years almost to the very beginning. I wanted the Valley to be a memorial, not only to the folks who had settled it but also to all those who had explored and settled and lived and labored in other valleys in the making of America. I thought how nice it would be if someday fifty or a hundred years from now folks could look upon it as a page in the history of their country and see here a picture that had faded out everywhere else. Renfro Valley, as I first saw it and best remembered it."

After farming, John Lair tried his hand at editing the newspaper in Corbin, Kentucky. He even tried his hand at politics, I'm told. And then he landed a job with Liberty Mutual Life Insurance Company, where he became one of their claim adjusters and was sent to their office in Boston. His job soon took him to Chicago. It was about this time that a student from his Mt. Vernon class, Virginia Crawford, be-came his new bride. They were married on June 8, 1924. He was now thirty years of age and starting a new life with a new wife and a new job. In spite of his homesickness, a better than average job and family responsibility kept him in Chicago with Liberty Mutual for the next ten years. Three of his four daughters were born during this time— Ann, Virginia Lee and Nancy. Barbara, the fourth daughter, was born in Berea, Kentucky.

This was the mid-twenties, and radio was trying to establish it-self across the country, and one of the nation's most powerful stations was WLS, the *Prairie Farmer* station. Whether it was Liberty Mutual business that brought John's attention to the station or just entertain-ment, for one reason or other, John Lair began to take notice of this new thing called radio. It offered a variety of entertainment. John was quick to notice that a little of it was a lot like the kind of music that he grew up with back in Renfro Valley. In fact, one of its performers was from back home or near home. His name was Bradley Kincaid. Brad-ley was the first of the ballad singers to bring his special music to radio.

John began to visit the radio station from time to time and be-came acquainted with some of the folks in charge of its operation. I guess if you can't go home, you bring some of home to you. That's what Mr. Lair set out to do when he invited two of the music makers

The Cumberland Ridge Runners as they first appeared at WLS in 1931. From the left: Slim Miller, Karl Davis, Doc Hopkins, Harty Taylor (Karl & Harty, the Renfro Valley Boys).

from Mt. Vernon to come to Chicago with the promise of a radio career. His scouting for talent was soon to pay off as others under his management were hired. To the team of Carl & Hardy, the Renfro Valley Boys, he added Doc Hopkins, another Rockcastle County boy; then an Indiana fiddler and comic, Slim Miller; and Hugh Cross and Gene Ruppe, organizing them under the name of the Cumberland Ridge Runners. For several years they appeared on the *WLS National Barn Dance*.

Another young man from back home, or near home at Berea, Kentucky, by the name of Clyde Julian Foley came to his attention. Red Foley, as Mr. Lair dubbed him, was in Mr. Lair's opinion the finest ballad singer he had ever heard. Yet, in spite of this, and though the station did give young Foley an audition, they would not put him on the payroll. Not to be outdone, John Lair added "Rambling" Red Foley playing the doghouse bass to his Cumberland Ridge Runners.

The first all-girl string band in radio. The original Coon Creek Girls with A'nt Idy, Daisy Lang, Violet Koehler, Lily May Ledford (in back), and Rosey Ledford. WCKY Radio announcer and A'nt Idy at the mike.

It seems the show bug that had been nibbling at John for so many years was now finally eating him alive. After ten years of making an honest living with Liberty Mutual, he was ready to gamble on a brand-new career. John Lair was in one way or the other all his life a communicator, teacher, cartoonist, poet, newspaper editor, and organizer. He saw in this new business of radio a chance to communicate ideas never before possible, and what better method than with the universal language of music?

Another that came under his management was a true mountain girl by the name of Lily May Ledford. With her in the lead, Mr. Lair would form the first all-girl band in radio, the Coon Creek Girls. A number of talented ladies would work with this group, including the Amburgey sisters—Irene, Opal and Bertha. However, from just a few years after its inception and until they disbanded in the late fifties, the members were Lily May and her sisters, Rosey and Minnie, better

Millie, Dolly, Red Foley, and Slim Miller in 1937. Front row: John Lair, an Owens A'nt Idy, and Little Clifford. Photo courtesy of Settles County Memorabilia.

known as Black-eyed Susie. A few recordings made were of this combination. Their biggest claim to fame came in the late thirties when they were included with a group of folksingers who were invited to the White House by President and Mrs. Roosevelt to sing for the King and Queen of England.

It's claimed that during the 1930s Mr. Lair was one of the earliest to use the bass fiddle and the Hawaiian guitar in hillbilly music. At a steel guitar convention in St. Louis a couple of years ago, Chubby

To Play At Fair. The cast of the "Renfro Valley Barn Dance," heard weekly over WLW, will broadcast from the coliseum at the State Fairgrounds at Columbus next Saturday night.

sister, the Duke of Paducah, the Coon Creek girls, Shug Fisher on bass fiddle,

Howard and Doc Lewis were talking with Jerry Byrd, who worked with Mr. Lair in the late thirties. When Jerry learned that Chubby and Doc were from the *Renfro Valley Show,* he was eager to share some of his memories. One had to do with an early morning radio show that he was on. Jerry and a number of the other cast members lived in nearby Berea and would drive down each morning, usually with enough time to run over a number or two before the show went on the air. Whether Jerry's trade for a new car the previous day had any-

Red Foley, Millie, and Dolly in 1939.

thing to do with them running late on this particular morning, I don't know, but they realized as they topped the hill going into the Valley that they would have no time to spare. Once they were parked, instruments would have to be taken from the car, rushed inside, taken from their cases. Fifteen seconds could make the difference between being on time or being too late. Jerry decided to do a few of the things in advance of arrival. First, he would put the car in neutral, take the keys from the ignition, then turn off Dixie Highway onto the lane that led to the Barn. He told the occupants to be ready for a sudden stop. They would open the doors, grab their instruments, and rush for the Barn. The only problem was, Jerry hadn't discovered one of the features of the new car. Once the key was taken from the ignition, the steering mechanism locked. Jerry and his passengers made it off Dixie Highway but not onto the lane that led to the Barn. They came to rest some distance out into the pasture field, to the amusement of those who were outside the barn watching and waiting. Jerry's graceful arrival made for a lot of friendly ribbing for more than just one morning program.

No matter what was going on in his newfound interest in the big city, Mr. Lair never forgot about home and reached out to it in every way that he could. The first sponsor for the Cumberland Ridge Runners on WLS was the Aladdin Lamp Company. Mr. Lair asked them to donate a couple of lights for the Rose Hill Church up Renfro Creek in Renfro Valley and also persuaded them to let him make the dedication by radio. Oscar Bryant of Mt. Vernon had a radio that he agreed to take out and set up in the church so they could invite the whole congregation to hear the broadcast. When the show went on the air that night from Chicago, the lights were up and burning and the neighbors were gathered in the little church in Renfro Valley. Few of them had ever listened to radio, and when John came on asking them to join in singing an old hymn from the hymn book in use at the church there was much excitement on both ends of the microphone.

This was an example of how he was able to bring the listener and the entertainer together in a way no one had done before. Another example is the Renfro Valley *Sunday Morning Gatherin'*. It went on the air for the first time in 1943 and is still heard today over more than two hundred radio stations across the United States and Canada. Mr. Lair often said on the *Sunday Morning Gatherin'* that a man spends the first half of his life trying to leave home and the last half trying to get back. At age forty-three, when his life was just about at its halfway mark, he started his journey back toward Renfro Valley.

The first stop after leaving Chicago in 1937 was Cincinnati, Ohio, where his cast of entertainers, now known as the Renfro Valley Folks, set up headquarters in the Cincinnati Music Hall for a Saturday night barn dance sponsored by the Keystone Steel and Wire Company, makers of Red Brand Fence. The cast included A'nt Idy and Little Clifford, Red Foley, Lily May Ledford, Shug Fisher, and the Coon Creek Girls, Slim Miller, Millie and Dolly Good, Bill Russell and his harmonica, Danny Duncan, the Callahan Brothers, and many more. John Lair needed another comedian and had heard about a fellow by the name of Whitey Ford, known as the Duke of Paducah, who was performing at a radio station in St. Louis, Missouri, and he'd sent word for the Duke to get in touch.

In 1972 we interviewed Whitey Ford for an article in our *Renfro*

Valley Bugle, and here's a little bit of what he had to say: "We were an instant hit in Cincinnati. We had every minute of our time sponsored and one portion of our show was on the NBC Blue network. The Red network was the big time and was the one that we were shooting for." He said, "This one year in Cincinnati established us as a country music show on the air and we were drawing tremendous crowds in theaters around the country. Things were moving so fast and so good John Lair decided to organize a company and buy land in Renfro Valley. The company was formed by John Lair; Red Foley; his brother, Cotton Foley; and Whitey Ford, the Duke of Paducah." Whitey said, "He knew that buying land would be difficult unless it was handled with kid gloves. I was appointed to be the Kid Glove Kid to do the job because I was not known to anyone around there." Whitey said he got the job done and before anyone had any idea of what was going on they owned the land and were ready to start building.

Whitey told us that he bought all the furniture, the bedding, the carpets for the cabins; all the equipment, pots, pans, the works, for the Lodge; and all the dishes, silverware, tablecloths for the dining room. Of course, before all the buying took place the buildings had to go up.

After a year in Cincinnati the show moved to Memorial Auditorium in Dayton, Ohio, for one year, and success continued to come their way.

The Beginning of the Valley Where Time Stands Still

Before they knew it, before they expected it to happen, the buildings were up in Renfro Valley. The Lodge, the tourist court and, of course, the big Show Barn. The Renfro Valley Folks were ready for their first performance of the *Renfro Valley Barn Dance* from the stage of the Old Barn in their new home at Renfro Valley. Whitey told us that Renfro Valley grew and prospered right from the start. They signed a lot of new talent, the barn was packed every Saturday night, and their road shows were breaking house records everywhere. Although the *Renfro Valley Barn Dance* was originating from the Old Barn in Renfro Valley, it was heard by the listening audience over radio station WLW in Cincinnati, where it had been heard since its first broadcast in October 1937. In spite of their success and in less than a year, the *Renfro Valley Barn Dance* lost its two biggest stars, the Duke of Paducah and Red Foley. Both came to the realization that if their careers were to blossom it had to be someplace else other than Renfro Valley. The Duke said, "I loved every minute of it and I gave it all I had but that little small voice inside me kept saying, this is not for you, or as the kids say today, this is not my bag." The little small voice was right. He said, "Freeman Keyes, the man who was in charge of the advertising company which was supplying all of our commercials, came to me and made me an offer. He said, 'Brown & Williamson Tobacco Company is going to start a full, NBC network show for Bugler Tobacco and they want you on it.' We agreed on the price, worked out a plan with John Lair for Mr. Keys to buy my Renfro Valley stock. I sold out and moved back to Chicago." We know that Red Foley left about this same time

Whitey Ford, the
"Duke of Paducah"

and headed back to Illinois, where he invested in his own dude ranch and again joined the *WLS National Barn Dance in Chicago.*

Now I have been told that Red believed he was misled by John Lair and Freeman Keyes as to the sponsorship of the program and radio time, believing they were in jeopardy, and because of that they sold out under unclear circumstances. Whether this is true or not, his leaving was to John's benefit. For what Mr. Lair had in mind, no partnership was workable. We have the script of that very first *Barn Dance,* and I'm wondering if John was sending Red a message in his introduction of him on that night. Quoting from the script, Mr. Lair said, "Now here is a young man who gave up his chance of fame and fortune in the big city to come down here in Renfro Valley and sing for you the kind of songs we know you love." Was he telling Red Foley if he wanted fame and fortune, he'd better go back to the city? It was a typical John Lair introduction, but I have an idea there was a hidden message there for Red.

This was the beginning of John Lair's "valley where time stands still." It was he who would originally impart the theme and personality to this little mountain village and source of entertainment. But if you thought he was building the valley of his dream, then you're wrong. The boyhood dream that he dreamed from that big rock topping the highest hill back of the home place, a dream that he called "foolishness that sometime or another comes to all boys, impossible dreams but hard to get rid of"—that dream would never be his. Look close at what he said. "A dream that sometime or other comes to all boys." Of course, we know all boys don't dream about Renfro Valley. He said he thought of what he would do if he had enough money to buy the whole valley some day. That's what all boys dream of; enough money to do what they want to do. He went on to say that his dream was not a conquest and advancement such as had inspired the early settlers in Renfro Valley to work hard and build up a settlement, the dream of progress and growth. He said his dream was in a way to move backward across the years almost to the very beginning. What was the very beginning? That's when the valley was practically a wilderness.

Now, you may have heard him on the *Gatherin'* describe the technicolor hills in the fall; the redbud and dogwoods in the spring; wild roses in the summer. He had more than just an eye for nature's beauty. His boyhood dream would be to return the valley to that wild but beautiful state. The valley that he was dreaming of would have had no paved roads, no service stations, no power lines, no tractors and tobacco fields, no big lodges or tourist courts, no log buildings with modern broadcast studios, and no big log homes with swimming pools and tennis courts, as his own home in Renfro Valley had. At the time he was dreaming these dreams, there was no such thing as radio, and commercial hillbilly music was unheard of. No, the little community he had built for himself in Renfro Valley was not a part of his original dream, but the dream would be a part of everything he would do from this point on.

Even if he had the means, I doubt if John Lair had the desire any longer to turn back the hands of time in Renfro Valley. With the combination of hillbilly music and radio, John Lair had found his niche in life. But the advancement of the Valley beyond what he had made it in 1939 was not in his plans either. So began the "valley where time stands still." Before the first anniversary, he was in full control. Although he had a financial partner, he alone set the tone of everything that went on on stage and off. To the casual observer, the *Renfro Valley Barn Dance* probably did not look or act much different than most of the other barn dances around the country, or should I say around the

The whole *Renfro Valley Barn Dance* crew, resting in the hayloft of the the Randolph Sisters, Gene Cobb, Jerry Byrd, Ernest Cornelison, and Elkins, Opal Ambergey, John Lair, Guy Blakeman, Jerry Behrens, Roland Cornelison, Shorty Hobbs, and Eller. Seated: Jethro Burns, Homer Harper, Little Clifford, A'nt Idy Harper, Douglas Spivey, Marvin Taylor,

cities, for in the beginning its rural location was the only thing that did set it apart from all the others.

By the time the first cast photos were taken, a number of new acts had been added to the original line-up. If radio stations were rosebushes, the hillbilly entertainers were the bees. They went from bush to bush. And Renfro Valley seemed to be offering something sweeter than all the rest.

Word had gone out that there was truly a new place to work and live in the country—a big time barn dance from where you could get national exposure and be heard on a 50,000-watt radio station. But they were soon to learn that Renfro Valley was not just your usual stop on the way to fame. And talent was not always enough. There was a standard that had to be met, and if you couldn't meet it in all

big barn between shows. Left to right, back row: Red Davis, Judy Dell, Aytchie Burns. Second row: Hartman Coffey, Buck Anderson, Henry Gaines, Geneva Powell, Margie Rambeau, Nancy Allen, Grace Haynes, Irene Amburgey, Lily May Ledford, Bertha Ambergey, Granny and Homer Miller.

respects, it was best you'd be on your way. More than one group regretted their audition for Renfro Valley. Seldom was a group hired, but many times an individual in the group was offered a position in Renfro Valley, which usually meant an end to the act. Name changes were common when you came to work at Renfro Valley. If John didn't think that your name had that right sound for the Renfro Valley stage, he would change it. For instance, Rickie Riddle became Wayne Turner, and Manuel "Speedy" Clark would not only change his name but his entire looks, make-up, and personality. Speedy became the character Old Joe Clark.

I once heard that Homer and Jethro, before joining the show in its first year, along with being accomplished musicians, were doing a sophisticated straight act. My friend James "Goober" Buchanan re-

Homer and Jethro.

cently told me that he was working with Homer and Jethro in their early days and that they did not like hillbilly music at all. But in spite of this, Mr. Lair presented these boys as bare-footed, overall-clad hillbillies while they were in Renfro Valley. We do know that after leaving the Valley they landed in Chicago, where once again they put class in their act and dress suits on their backs and became nationally known for their parodies of pop music hits. John Lair wanted no cowboys on the stage; it was okay for the trio or quartet to do from time to time old western classics, but no flashy cowboy clothes or modern cowboy songs; it did not fit the image of a Kentucky mountain music show. The material on the *Barn Dance* was made up mostly of songs of tragic romance, novelty, gospel, and story songs. The commercial cheating songs that came along and were so popular on record would only occasionally find their way to the *Barn Dance* microphone and then that would be determined by the contents of the song, not by its popularity. John Lair was using his talent as script writer and narrator to tell the world that here in the Kentucky hills on the edge of the Cumberland Mountains was a place of frolic, fun, and sacred tranquility. With word pictures he painted the Valley as a place shut away from the outside world, where the way of life moved at such a pace that it could be called the "valley where time stands still."

WHAS had become the station of the *Barn Dance,* and Ballard & Ballard of Louisville, Kentucky, was one of the new sponsors making possible a number of daily broadcasts. The Lodge Restaurant was the setting for an early-morning program sponsored by Ballard's Obelisk Flour. Later in the morning, two or three more programs would originate from the Lodge and the Old Barn stage. The forties were John's most successful decade. In addition to the two or three Saturday night *Barn Dance* performances, there were three and four daily broadcasts Monday through Friday and the *Renfro Valley Gatherin'* on Sunday morning. Personal appearances throughout the East, Northeast, and South were at their peak. The power of network radio in the wartime years was nothing less than awesome.

I wasn't in Renfro Valley, but at the age of fourteen, in 1945, I was in radio for my first time. My group, the Pine Valley Pals, were packing them in at the little one- and two-room schoolhouses within the listening distance of WHOP in Hopkinsville, Kentucky. I can just imagine what the *Barn Dance* talent was doing. In addition to appearances in school auditoriums, civic centers, and the theater circuit, there were two and three tent show units going out from the Valley, sometimes staying six months at a time. There was talent that worked the tent shows that never made it to the *Barn Dance* stage in Renfro Valley. I have just recently learned that Cowboy Copas was on the tent circuit for a while even though he was never a member of the *Barn Dance* cast, never making an appearance in the Valley.

I was not aware of the name on the marquee or even the name of the show, but I have every reason to believe that the first Renfro Valley performance I ever saw was under the big top in a little western Kentucky town when I was around thirteen or fourteen years of age. It was the music and the singing I went to hear, but it was the comedy and the magic of an act I have since determined was the Happy Homes Fun Show that captured my attention. This act shared the bill with Renfro Valley. The tent show performers were not billed as the *Renfro Valley Barn Dance,* just John Lair's Renfro Valley Folks. And during those days there were two and three units traveling out of Renfro Valley.

I recently ran across some information on one of the units I be-

Tent Show Poster

lieve might have been considered the main unit, under the direction of Gene "Nubbin" Cobb. Ralph Grubbs, one of the entertainers, kept a log on the 1946 season and, according to his information, the big 80 foot by 180 foot canvas theater tent was owned by a William Ketrow. The tent and tour dates were managed by the Ketrow family; Robert Ketrow shared the announcing duties with Gene Cobb and the handling of mail and route cards with Happy Homes. Hazel Cobb and Viola Grubbs, wives of the performers, were two of the ticket sellers, while Gene Cobb and the Ketrow family members handled the collection of tickets. Soft drinks, sandwiches, prize candy, and popcorn were handled by another five-member staff. Another crew of three were in maintenance; a canvas crew of six put up and took down the big tent after each performance.

In the year 1946, the first week in May, the Renfro Valley Folks headed out in trucks, cars and trailers; twenty-five in all when the show finally rendezvoused in Lumberton, North Carolina, for the first performance on Monday, May 6. On May 7, they set up tent for another one-nighter just thirty miles on over the road in Laurenberg, North

Carolina. The dates were anywhere from twenty-five to sixty-five miles apart; some were as close as eleven and twelve miles from the previous performance. From North Carolina, where they had shown in ten ball parks, fairgrounds, and vacant lots, they went into Virginia for fourteen like performances. Sunday, June 2, was their first day off, if you call driving from Romany, West Virginia, to Westport, Maryland, a day off.

From the state of Maryland it was into Pennsylvania and then to Conneaut, Ohio, for a date on Monday, June 17, that was then canceled, the only cancellation on the entire tour and for what reason I never learned. Soon they were playing in nine states with twice as many dates in the state of Michigan as any of the others. Of the 134 towns visited, 59 were with our good friends in the state of Michigan. The show was on the road for twenty-two weeks. They played 123 one-night stands, 9 two–day stands, and 1 three–day stand in Lansing, Michigan, where they were butting heads with Ringling Brothers Barnum & Bailey's Circus and where they drew their smallest crowd of only 470 people on one of those three nights.

With a tent seating capacity of 1,800, in twenty-two weeks they showed to an estimated crowd of 1,470,000; the largest for any show was 2,179 at West Jefferson, North Carolina, on the second week of their tour, Thursday, May 16.

This troupe included Miss Patty Flye, who along with her sister, Betty, came to Renfro Valley shows at a very young age. The marriage of her sister broke up that act, and she teamed with Iza May Courtwright and began touring with the Gene Cobb tent performers. She was one of the performers who would make her way from the tent shows back to the *Barn Dance* and be around for a good many years. Patty was a fine vocalist and accordion player. There was Shorty Bradford, who was billed as "The Man With Two Voices"; the Jostus Sisters, Pauline and Mildred, were featured hymn singers with the Renfro Valley Show; vocalist Glenn Ferguson played guitar and fiddle; Buddy Nelson strummed a mean guitar and sang a fine song, according to the billing. Gene Cobb, according to his publicity, was married but had nothing running around the house but a little picket fence, started in show business with a song and dance team known as Phelps, Columbine and Cobb. A solo fling at vaudeville, musical comedy and minstrel shows finally led him to the Renfro Valley stage. And there was Ralph Grubbs, or Ralph Ross, as he was billed, playing the mandolin and enjoying his fifteen minutes of Renfro Valley fame more than anyone I've ever known. Ralph is best remembered for his crying rendition of "Blue Eyes." These folks closed out their last date Sunday, October 6, in Logan, Ohio, packed up and headed for the barn in Renfro Valley.

There is a section of Mt. Vernon called Fairground Hill. It's a residential area now, but in the forties it was a place set aside for fairs, carnivals, tent shows, and the like. In a display at the edge of the stage of the New Barn auditorium there's an old aluminum bass fiddle, of all things, that came to Renfro Valley by way of a traveling minstrel tent show that played Mt. Vernon at Fairground Hill.

On the show was a young comic, emcee, and trumpet player by the name of Gabe Tucker. John Lair had heard about Gabe and went out to see if he could hire him for the *Renfro Valley Barn Dance*, as he was in bad need of an emcee at the time. They struck a deal, and Gabe agreed to stay on in Renfro Valley when the show left town. Because of a windstorm, the show moved on a little ahead of schedule; the storm left their tent and other equipment in shambles. The following day, Gabe Tucker and Mr. Lair went up to see the damage and to try to salvage some chairs. When they rolled back the tent, there lay the old bass fiddle, untouched, or at least undamaged by the storm. I'm told that Gabe Tucker was one of the finest emcees Renfro Valley has ever had. He left the *Barn Dance* in the late forties for a colorful career with many of the big stars of the fifties and sixties, including Elvis Presley. He left Renfro Valley Folks an aluminum bass fiddle and a hatfull of memories.

An entertainer didn't have to be in Renfro Valley too long to find out that there was no place on the *Barn Dance* for an individual star. It would be this policy that would turn out to have a more negative effect on talent than anything else. There would be some who would blame John Lair for holding them back. They would wonder what they could have done had they had the freedom to promote their careers as was done at the Grand Ole Opry in Nashville. Even the Coon Creek Girls, especially Lily May, looked back with some regret. But no one was forced to stay. In fact when an act did leave, they were in most cases welcomed back when they wanted to return. A lot of talent came across the Renfro Valley stage during the heyday of radio. Only after radio dropped the use of live talent did the cast settle down to a regular crew who stayed more than two or three years. Old Joe Clark just recently celebrated fifty years in show business, and most all of those years were spent at Renfro Valley's *Barn Dance*. Most entertainers who have worked at Renfro Valley for any length of time looked back on that time with fond memories.

The *Barn Dance* has always been the entertainer's show. It offered a chance to walk in front of the very best audience in the world and to work with the cream of the crop. But, as in so many cases, you couldn't have it all. At Renfro Valley you could have the fun and frolic, but you couldn't have the fame or the fortune.

There's a story that comes with every picker, singer, or comedian that has made a trip on and off the Renfro Valley stage. Each one was different in enough ways to have been remembered individually, but each one similar in enough ways that many times we'll refer to them as the Renfro Valley Folks. History failed to record much of anything of national prominence about the Valley after the forties had come and gone. Oh, its beginning has been told and retold a number of times over the years. After that, like a fading star, Renfro Valley was just around and that was about all. But even that in itself could be counted a success story as most all the other country music shows that may have outshone the *Barn Dance* in popularity for a short time were soon to die out completely.

The things that set the *Barn Dance* apart in the beginning were the things that gave it its longevity. It catered to true entertainers and entertainment rather than to commercial music. All the other shows were owned by broadcast stations and big corporations, and decisions were made by a board of directors, but Renfro Valley was a one-man operation and, for most of its first fifty years, John Lair was that man. I feel that John Lair's contributions to country music certainly qualify him for induction into the Country Music Hall of Fame. His efforts were self-serving, for sure, but that doesn't make them any less important. The *Renfro Valley Barn Dance* never tried to be a poor man's Grand Ole Opry as many of the other country shows succeeded in being. Most of the talent on our stage were and are original, not wannabes and mimics. It was for this reason you could work the *Barn Dance* with pride even though the Valley may have been seeing some hard times along the way.

For almost ten years there was very little expansion in Renfro Valley except to Mr. Lair's home and his private property. After the Lodge and the Old Barn were completed in 1939, it wasn't until about 1947 that the big, log museum building was nearly ready for occupancy. This building might be considered the compromise to Mr. Lair's dream. If he couldn't own the entire valley as a pioneer museum, he would cram as much of its past into this building as possible. His pioneer museum occupied the top floor of this massive, log structure. But it was much more than just a museum. It was John Lair's private office, ticket office, and bookkeeper's department. A back room was added as a rec room for the talent, but it was soon taken over for various other projects. This room was home to the *Renfro Valley Bugle* for a good many years. And for a good many years it was known as the kitchen as it had a sink and a hot plate. It was converted into the office of the director of entertainment in 1990.

The building featured a breezeway down the middle of the first floor. The offices I just mentioned were on the left side of the breezeway as you entered the front of the building. On the right side were the broadcast studios where many of the daily programs originated. And this building was the winter home of the *Renfro Valley Sunday Morning Gatherin'* program. These facilities were first class in every respect. The main studio, or "big studio" as it is referred to, displayed the oil paintings of such folk artists as Bradley Kincaid, Bascom Lamar Lunsford, John Jacob Niles, and of course, John Lair. One mystery, at least for me, is the empty frame on one wall. Whose picture was this frame intended to hold, and why wasn't it completed? Studios were equipped for broadcast by the engineers at WHAS radio station in Louisville, Kentucky. It was the same studios that would become home to Renfro Valley's little radio station in later years.

The breezeway of this old building holds some fond memories for me. I recall a time after the *Barn Dance* one Saturday night, late enough that we all should have been home in bed. Vester Parker, Al Ballinger, Bee Lucas, one or two of the other band members, and myself were in the parking area between the old barn and the museum building. I got into Vester Parker's Volkswagen. I had been talking trade with Vester, and I thought I would try it out. I drove it around the museum along the side that was sitting on a bank just barely wide enough for a Volkswagen to go around. When I reached the front of the building, that put me out on the front lawn. Rather than cross the lawn any more than I had to I thought, "Well, I'll go down the breezeway; a good solid rock floor, no damage can be done and after all, no one will ever know." Well, that's just what I thought. The next morning we were there for the *Sunday Morning Gatherin'*. John Lair drove up, got out of his car, came to the breezeway, stopped dead in his tracks. Well, what he had to say wasn't in the *Gatherin'* script, I can tell you that. There they were, just as plain as the nose on your face. The grass the night before had been wet with dew and those tire tracks down the center of the breezeway were as if they had been painted there. John ran his fingers through his hair, looked me right in the eye, and he said, "I want you to look—somebody has been driving an automobile through my building!" All I could think of to say was, "I think Vester Parker has a car like that." As far as I know, nothing else was ever mentioned about it. Just to be on the safe side, I put off trading for that Volkswagen for about six months.

I want to share a story with you now that Emory Martin told me a few years ago. In 1947, in addition to the new pioneer museum building, a little record factory opened in a building that stood right where the New Barn auditorium stands today. Mr. Lair's partner in this venture was a gentleman from Kansas who owned some record-pressing equipment, and they operated under the name of Ekko Recording Corporation of Renfro Valley, Kentucky. Ekko pressed for the Radio label, which was possibly owned by this same corporation. In the seventies we found a stack of unsold records (all by Doc Hopkins, a WLS artist, according to the label) still in their original box. The label was blue and pictured a microphone with the word Radio and stated that the record was for use on home phonographs. Side A was "The Blue Tail Fly." Side B was Doc Hopkins playing "Cripple Creek."

The Ekko Recording Corporation wasn't in business but for a short while. I just recently learned that it was John Lair's fear that their recording business and record label would bring the musicians union into the Valley and so he discontinued recording. When they moved out, another business moved in, this time the Walnut Factory, which evidently was around a little bit longer because this building became known as the walnut factory. Folks in the community and the surrounding area would bring in their walnuts, and machinery would hull, dry, crack, and separate the kernels from the shells and package them for sale. After this business folded, the building became a storage area.

We are now accustomed to stars pulling in for their concerts in big, long, shiny buses—complete homes on wheels. Long before this was a custom, the *Renfro Valley Show* traveled in a bus. This bus, I've been told, would take the Renfro Valley Folks on tours from theater to theater, town to town, state to state, between flat tires, dead batteries, locked starters, flooding carburetors, leaking heaters and flat brakes. I've heard from more than one entertainer about this bus, although I don't think I've ever heard it referred to as a bus. They've called it everything else, but never a bus. One told me about the time they were on this contraption in Washington, D.C., going around in circles trying to get off of a highway onto one they could plainly see just across a little grassy knoll, but they could not find an exit. Around and around they went. Finally the driver, losing patience and with a few choice words of disgust, took a shortcut across the grassy knoll and onto the highway home. Can't you just see that happening this day and time?

Well, I said all that to say all this: Emory was telling me about a time when he was traveling home by car from a personal appearance tour and as they got near the Rockcastle County line they saw a light on the horizon that indicated there was a big fire under way some-place up ahead. They first thought of their homes in nearby Mt. Vernon. By the time they got to the Mt. Vernon city limits, it was obvious that the fire was a little further out and in the direction of Renfro Valley, and, of course, their first thought went to the big Old Barn. A fire this size just had to be the Old Barn. Instead of heading home as they normally would, they headed out to the Valley to find out what was going on. They were soon able to see that the fire was beyond the Old Barn and learned that it was the walnut factory that was burning, a building less than one-third the size of the barn, but all those old walnut hulls scattered around were making quite a fire. They got out of their car, walked toward the building, where a crowd had gathered. And right away they recognized the silhouette of Old Joe Clark be-tween them and the blaze. As they approached Old Joe, he was heard to say in a low but firm voice, "Burn, you SOB, burn." On further inquiry they learned that the SOB Joe was referring to was that old bus someone had left parked inside the building. I know Joe hated that bus bad enough to burn it, but I really don't think he had any-thing to do with it.

Ralph Grubbs had already done his thing in Renfro Valley and left by the time I got here, but while living in nearby Danville, Ken-tucky, I've had the pleasure of talking with Ralph a number of times. Ralph was not in the music business before coming to Renfro Valley and chose to get out after his job in Renfro Valley was over. But he observed more of what went on during his few years in Renfro Valley than anyone that I've met.

I remember a story he told me about running into Mr. Lair one day after a meeting Mr. Lair had had with Freeman Keyes, his financial partner. Keyes, you will remember, was the one who had earlier purchased Red Foley and Whitey Ford's shares in Renfro Valley. Exactly what those shares were, I don't know. The incident I'm speaking of happened in the late forties. Mr. Lair walked out of the meeting with Keyes and ran into Ralph on his way into the Valley. With a big smile on his face, John walked up to Ralph and said, "I have just made the deal of a lifetime." He said Mr. Lair held up one finger and said, "I have just purchased the whole Renfro Valley settlement for $1." Just why Keyes made this generous offer we may never know for sure. Could be this time, like Red and Whitey, it was he who now heard that little small voice telling him it was time to go.

Ralph also told me a story about Fairly Holden, Renfro Valley's hottest act. Fairly was a singer of novelty songs, and he had a way with the ladies. And there were always a good many of them at the show who came just to see and listen to Fairly Holden. Long before there was an Elvis, there was Fairly. Now, he was not a great singer. I don't even know if you would consider him a good singer, but he was a great entertainer and, like I say, he did have a way with the ladies. And evidently John Lair recognized the commercial value in Fairly, for, as I understand it, he allowed him to make a whopping $250 a week there for a while, almost twice as much as anyone else was reported to have been making. One of his hottest stage numbers was a song John had written called "Keep Them Cold Icy Fingers Off of Me." Well, things were going good for him, better than I suppose he ever thought they would go. Here he was on the popular Renfro Valley *Barn Dance,* had a hit song on his hands, and what do you do in a case like that? Why you do what comes naturally, you take advantage of it while the getting is good. That's exactly what Fairly did. The crowds loved him and if his pay was any indication, so did the boss. He could do no wrong, so he thought, so poor Fairly forgot about Rule Number One. Whether he went seeking an agent and a recording contract or whether they came to him, I don't know. But the deal must have moved pretty fast because he was in Cincinnati recording with King Records before anyone knew about it.

Fact of the matter is, Chubby Howard just told me a little bit about the recording session. King's recording equipment was set up in a warehouse. It was the wintertime and mighty cold. They had to just keep doing it over and over and over, and finally Fairly said, "I don't know if I can do this anymore, I'm losing my voice." One of the musicians spoke up and said, "Fairly, you don't have a voice to lose."

But he did have a song and a way with the ladies, and that's all it took. He recorded John's "Keep Them Cold Icy Fingers Off of Me," signed with an agent, and headed back to Renfro Valley, where we pick up the story in the Lodge Restaurant as Fairly is making his entrance.

John Lair's office was upstairs over the Lodge at the time. Fairly comes in and there are two or three of the entertainers, Ralph Grubbs one of them, at the table having coffee. Fairly walks over, all excited, and says, "Boys, you'll never believe what's happened; I just recorded with King Records and I have me an agent and I'm on my way." He couldn't wait to get upstairs to tell his boss about it. Ralph said Fairly just bounced up the stairs. He wasn't up there more than 30 seconds when they heard a loud bang from the direction of Mr. Lair's office. In a little while, Fairly came downstairs minus his smile and his face drained of all its color. He walked up to the table and he said, "He fired me; John Lair has fired me." The bang they had heard was John's fist coming down on his desk when Fairly told him that he had signed with an agent and had recorded for King. I suppose in his case he had reason to believe that his career had been held back a mite. Rule Number One—you don't record anything or sign with anyone but John Lair. I believe John rehired Fairly before the week was up, but the honeymoon was over and so were his $250-a-week paydays.

A story from the forties I got during one of our reunions came from a couple of the ladies, Mary Randolph and Patty Flye. Patty was about fifteen or sixteen years old, I suppose; Mary, a little older and a little wiser, took Patty under her wing, looking out for her at least while they were on the road. In this instance, they were in a little town out of state, a week's engagement at a little county fair. After one of the performances, Patty and Mary went out on the midway of the carnival section of the fair to pass the time and to see what was happening. They passed a girlie show, and Mary suggested they go in. She told Patty she always wondered what went on in one of those shows. Well, Patty really didn't think that they should go in because they might see something they shouldn't see, but Mary reasoned that they were away from home and no one knew them there, so why not get a little education? Patty reluctantly said okay, bought the tickets and they went in the tent, which was practically empty. The show was under way, the girls were on stage, and as soon as they found their seats, they glanced around nervously to see what was going on with the other patrons. Sure enough, right away they saw something they

A'nt Idy and Little Clifford.

shouldn't have seen. In seats a few rows ahead of them, they recognized Wade Baker, Randall Parker, Slim Miller and John Lair.

A'nt Idy and Little Clifford was Renfro Valley's most publicized comedy act of the early forties, a team that was short-lived due to the untimely death of A'nt Idy, its main character. I had the opportunity to work with Little Clifford, or Harry Mullins as I knew him, not as an entertainer but Harry as John Lair's nephew. When I came to Renfro Valley, Harry already had taken on the role of Renfro Valley's purchasing agent, ticket taker, and booking agent for some of the talent. And he assigned himself another position, that of advertising agent, it seems.

If you have ever looked closely at the Old Barn or a picture of the Old Barn or a print of the oil painting of the Old Barn, you may have

Last Cast Picture. Reading left to right: Norma Coffey, Lily May and Minnie Flye, Virginia Sutton, and Elsie Behrens. Back row: Birdsee Haycraft, Tommy Holden, John Lair, Al Staas, Bob Simmons, Glen Pennington, Wade Baker,

wondered why up in the left hand corner of one side of the building there's about a 10 foot by 14 foot section painted yellow. Well, you can credit this to Harry Mullins, I'm told. It seems that Harry, or "Wad" as he was nicknamed, decided one day that that big Old Barn would be a wonderful place to advertise some of the things Renfro Valley had to offer. Now, I don't know when this decision was made, but the action on it took place one week when Mr. John Lair was away on business. Harry knew his Uncle John as well or better than anyone and he must have known how much he hated paint, paint of any kind on anything. I remember how long it took him to finally agree just to put a sealer on the outside of the Barn in order to preserve it. I suppose the great advertising possibilities of a big sign on the side of the barn clouded Harry's judgment. We'll never know what Harry planned to say on his big billboard, for John Lair made it back before the lettering went on, but not before this great big yellow blotch was painted on those hallowed boards. I can well imagine John's reaction to this

Ledford, Flossie Thomas, Jean Dickerson, Little Eller, Judy Dickerson, Patty Covington, Ruel Thomas, Lloyd Davidson, Roy Davidson, Smoky Ward, Fairly Jerry Behrens, and Troy Gibbs.

blunder that couldn't be fixed short of tearing down the wall. I'm sure he forgave Harry, but I don't suppose he could ever forget, for every time he entered the Valley, there was Harry's big bright yellow idea staring down at him. It can still be seen faintly on the Old Barn.

What has been called the biggest blunder in Renfro Valley's history took place in the late forties and was credited to John Lair himself. It had to do with his taking the Renfro Valley Shows to Florida for the winter, against the advice of friends and business associates. It seems he was told well in advance of the move that the sponsor, Ballard & Ballard, was against it and would cancel their contract if he followed through with it. In spite of this warning, John Lair, the *Barn Dance* and *Gatherin'* casts packed up and headed for the Florida sunshine for the winter. When they returned in the spring, the Valley was right there where they'd left it, but, true to their word, Ballard & Ballard had packed up their biscuits and gone home.

A number of times I have heard this story told by the entertainers who were in the Valley at the time, told in disbelief that anyone would be so dumb. Lily May used to say he did it because he was just too bull-headed. I never gave it much thought until recently when one of those veterans of the forties was telling me about Freeman Keyes and his ties to the Valley. Remember, Freeman was the one who bought Red Foley and Whitey Ford's interests in Renfro Valley Folks and became a partner of John Lair. But Freeman's main interest was that of salesman. He was responsible for the first sponsor, Keystone Fence, Brown & Williamson Tobacco Company, and others, and when these sponsors dropped out, it was Freeman who brought in Ballard & Ballard. And for his efforts, he was getting a whopping 25 percent of the sales, which was at least 10 percent above the normal commission. Freeman had a number of other network shows to his credit at the time, *The Red Skelton Show* for one.

I'm sure Mr. Lair looked upon this 25 percent as money that should be going into his own pocket, and we know he was never comfortable with a partner, even one who stayed out of the limelight as Freeman seemed to do. Now, John Lair was known to be a little bull-headed, made a few mistakes along the way, but he was not dumb at any time. I think he needed to rid himself of a partner. What better way than to take away his income by playing foolish and by losing the Ballard & Ballard account? John Lair was no longer obligated to Mr. Keyes. Was he counting on getting them back by himself? Was it just luck that a young Tom Wood was waiting in the wings, or did John Lair know he was there all along? Just speculation, of course, but hindsight tells us that we might not be very far from wrong.

Yes, the forties were good years, and when they came to a close in Renfro Valley the door began to close on an era in country music show business that has not and more than likely will never come again.

1950 to 1960

Entertainers of the Changing Times

The *Barn Dance* was well into its eleventh year before I learned there was such a show, and two more years went by before I got the opportunity to be a part of it. As much fun as it would have been to have been a part of those first thirteen years, I much more prefer to have been a part of the past thirteen and now, in my forty-seventh year, I'm looking forward to the future. Since I have had an opportunity to work with so many of the entertainers who were here in the beginning, I feel as if I've had the best of both worlds.

In addition to John Lair, Slim Miller was around for about ten years of my early tenure and was a character off stage as well as on. Slim had the reputation of being able or willing to talk about anything, anywhere, anytime. No matter what subject might come up, Slim knew a little bit about it. Slim had been there and done that. Someone who had worked with Slim for a number of years had been keeping record and one day told him, "Slim, according to what you've done and where you've been, you've got to be at least five hundred years old."

Ralph Grubbs recently passed on some Slim Miller stories. He said you could never catch Slim in the wrong. He remembered the time when they were on a road show, a little *Barn Dance* unit that was playing out down south, and Slim was the fiddler, comedian and, in this case, the driver for at least a portion of the trip. As they left Memphis, someone in the car thought they might be taking the wrong route and pointed this out to Slim. Slim didn't respond but just kept driving. Soon, someone else mentioned that they were sure they were on

Theater Crowd.

the wrong road. Still, Slim made no comment, just kept driving. Then a road sign up ahead confirmed their suspicions that they were on the wrong road. Still, Slim just kept driving until he came to a service station. He pulled into the pumps, the attendant came out and Slim asked, "Is Bill here?" The attendant asked, "Who?" Slim said, "Bill, Bill Smith. Doesn't Bill work here anymore?" "No," said the attendant, "I don't even know a Bill Smith." Slim, acting disgusted, pulled out of the service station onto the road and went back in the direction that they'd come, claiming he drove out that far just to say hello to his old friend, Bill Smith, who didn't have the courtesy to tell him that he had quit his job.

Lily May and the Coon Creek Girls were still very much at the center of things when I arrived. The Coon Creek Girls I first knew as a group were Lily May, Rosey, and Black-eyed Susie. Granny Harper, the little, short, stooped, pipe-smoking, bonnet-clad, gravel-voiced dancer, fiddler, and harmonica player was very much a part of the *Barn Dance* and road shows for my first year or two. Joe Clark wasn't on the show when I signed on in January 1952. He had been there for a while but had left to work with Bill Monroe among others, and he came back sometime in '53, I believe. The reason I mention Joe right here is because of his relationship with Granny Harper. Granny was in her seventies, I suppose, and I guess Manuel Clark was around, oh, his late twenties, as "Speedy" Clark. Granny could not stand him. She didn't want anything to do with him, didn't want to be in the room with him. But when "Speedy" put on his beard, his white hair, mustache, and his Old Joe Clark costume, Granny just loved that old codger. Speedy couldn't wait to get out of that makeup so she could despise him again. Too bad Granny is not around today, since "Speedy" finally grew into the Old Joe character.

I enjoyed the talents of Jerry Behrens. His career had gone through a number of changes by the time we shared the stage together. He first joined the *Barn Dance* as a member of a western group. His work at Renfro Valley included his part with the Mountain Rangers, a trio that also included Guy Blakeman and Roland Gaines. After his marriage to Elsie of the Randolph Sisters (Elsie and Jane), they became quite popular as a sweetheart duet. Jerry was also a member of the Rusty Gate Quartet, but it was as a soloist on such numbers as "Danny Boy" and "Old Folks at Home" that he really showed his talents as a vocalist.

He was a devoted fan of Stephen Foster. I found this out the hard

Cast of the 1952 Renfro Valley road show. Back row: Emory Martin (Old Joe Clark stand in) Claud Sweet. Front row: Pete Stamper, Speedy Clark, Glen Pennington.

way. In my comedy routine I sang a parody of Foster's "Beautiful Dreamer" and still do now and then. I really butcher the lyrics, and the first time Jerry heard me do this, he got highly insulted. In fact, the next time I did it, he left the stage, all this without my knowledge until someone told me, I think it was Black-eyed Susie, that Jerry just didn't think it was at all funny. I didn't quit doing the song, but I slowed up a mite.

Ray Sosby was the violinist on the *Barn Dance* and the *Gatherin'*. I always thought Ray looked and played more like a violinist than a

Lair at the microphone

fiddler. Dick Dickerson played steel guitar. It was Renfro Valley, but Dick played as hot a steel guitar as I've ever heard played on any show. Wayne Turner was one of the lead vocalists. Glen Pennington was bass player, bass singer in the Rusty Gate Quartet, and master of ceremonies of the stage portion of the *Renfro Valley Barn Dance*.

After his brother, Lloyd, left the show, Roy Davidson teamed up with Claud Sweet. Claud and Roy had some great harmony, especially on those good, old country blues numbers, the kind of songs that made the Delmore Brothers famous. Rounding out the entertainers were Emory Martin, one-armed banjo player, and his pretty wife, Linda Lou, playing the fiddle and steel guitar. Linda Lou and Emory both had fun at what they were doing.

The man who saw to it that we got our programs on and off the air on time was engineer Virgil Mann. He made sure the remote equipment was working right and both microphones were in place. One mike was on a stand at the center of the stage, connected to the four big morning-glory speakers that hung above the stage, and one, lowered on a rope down from the rafters of the stage, carried the sound of the *Barn Dance* to the listening audience of WLW in Cincinnati and WHAS in Louisville, Kentucky.

My $25 per week for doing one show and a honeymoon cabin to live in didn't seem bad compared to the $60 my friend Junior DeFore made for his two performances, considering he had to travel round-trip from Villa Rica, Georgia, every weekend to be on the *Renfro Valley Barn Dance* and the *Sunday Morning Gatherin'*. Junior was a great

41

The Callaway sisters: Clara, Coleida, and Sudie.

influence on me as a musician. After I heard him play the mandolin as only he could, I decided to give it up. His talents are captured forever on the recordings of *The Country Store* program still offered for sale in the Renfro Valley Music Store.

And then there were the Callaway sisters: Sudie, Coleida, and Clara, three pretty young ladies from the coal mining camp of Harlan County. They were living with Jerry Behrens and his family in the Valley. Those girls sure loved swimming in Renfro Creek. I didn't like swimming all that much, but I did like the Callaway sisters. I never spent so much time in the water in my life. I'll always remember their version of "Ghost Riders in the Sky." The girls now have successful careers as back-up singers in Nashville. These are the Renfro Valley Folks I first met and worked with, the ones that took the Renfro Valley show out of the radio heydays of the forties into the good, bad, and ugly days of the fifties.

My small part in those years were the best and worst of my Renfro Valley experiences. My years to learn and enjoy working with professional entertainers in big-time show business were 1952 and 1953. They gave me the opportunity to meet another of the Valley's founders; the one man in country music I admired most; the one I had been listening to on radio for so long. To leave Renfro Valley for a job with none other than Red Foley was almost more than I could believe. I remember when I told Mr. Lair that I was leaving and who I was leaving with, he gave Red credit for being a fine singer and good entertainer but cautioned me that he was "tight" with his money. He made leaving easier by telling me that if it didn't work out, to come on back.

Days of Big-Time Radio

The fifties brought something brand new for Renfro Valley, General Foods on the CBS network. This was to the credit of a young man by the name of Tom Wood, a New York advertising executive who had roots in Rockcastle County. In Tom's own words, he explained it like this: "At the age of twenty-seven with no experience whatsoever, I quit my job in the advertising department at General Foods in New York and six months later I sold the entire sponsorship of Renfro Valley back to my friends at General Foods. It was a $1 million package consisting of three broadcasts, the Saturday night *Barn Dance*, the *Sunday Morning Gatherin'*, and the *Country Store* program five times a week. It was the largest radio package sold in 1950. Perhaps one of the reasons for our success in selling the time to the New York advertising agency was the unusual presentation. I used what was then the first consumer tape recorder. It was so new that no one in the advertising agency or prospective clients had ever seen one. And when at the conference table at our presentation I said, 'Let's go down to Renfro Valley and hear John Lair.' And just like a radio, I leaned over the table and turned on the tape recorder, and the effect on the advertising people was amazing."

The tape recorder got attention, but John Lair held onto it with the pictures he painted in the imagination of those listeners, a picture of life and times in Renfro Valley as only John Lair could describe it. A portion of that very recording is now a part of the audio portion of the John Lair theater presentation. Yes, that sale to CBS and General Foods was great. It carried Renfro Valley into the fifties in style.

This book is not the Pete Stamper Story, but I would like to relate, for personal reasons if none other, the events that turned me in the direction of Renfro Valley. After graduation from high school in 1948, I volunteered for the army, agreeing for a year's service and six years in the reserve. I did this to prevent my being drafted and taking three years out of my show business plans, which I didn't think that I could afford. When my year was over with Uncle Sam in 1949, I came home and teamed up with my partner in comedy, long-time friend Clarence Williams, and we set out on what we hoped would be a long and successful career. We sought the services of an old showman from Paducah, Kentucky, who had retired and was selling cars in that city. His name was Uncle Billy Woods, and together we went on our radio broadcast in Madisonville, Kentucky. Things just didn't work out. Uncle Billy wasn't as interested in getting back into show business as he thought he was. We were there long enough to make the acquaintance of a young man, Curly Meyers, who had a program on the station along with his brother, brother-in-law, and sister. Curly took a liking to us, as they say, and invited us to join his show, and things seemed to be going real good. I was about ten months into my civilian career when suddenly I received a notice from Uncle Sam that the war in Korea had taken a turn for the worse, the Chinese had entered the fight, and my services were once again needed. I was to report right away for induction, after which I would be allowed to come home for about thirty days to get my affairs in order before reporting for permanent duty.

Now, I mention all this to explain the frame of mind I was in when I arrived at Ft. Campbell, Kentucky, to receive my orders. I could not imagine anything worse than what was happening to me. For the first time in my show business career, things had been going great. And suddenly it was all over, possibly never to be again. I was part of a team, and my buddy, I reasoned, couldn't sit around and wait for me to whip all of China. He was a fine soloist, and I wasn't sure if he would even need a partner by the time I made it back. These were some of the things that were going through my mind or at least these were things I was feeling as I made up my bunk in the barracks to which I had been assigned. To say I was down in spirits would be an understatement. I felt lower than I ever thought I would or could be. They say that misery loves company, but, in this case, I wanted to be alone. So I walked out the door of the barracks to take a stroll around the camp trying to come to terms with my situation.

I hadn't much more than stepped off the barrack steps when I heard a voice that got my attention. My first thought was that it was a voice I recognized. Possibly, someone from my hometown or maybe someone I had served in the service with just the year before. I couldn't hear the conversation, but I looked in the direction the sound was coming from. I saw a group of men, four or five, sitting around under a tree. I searched their faces and realized they were all strangers to me. As I began to walk away, that voice spoke once more. And it was at this moment, this split-second, that I went against every feeling I had in me except perhaps a tiny bit of curiosity. Instead of walking on out into loneliness as I had planned, I changed direction, stepped off the walk, and walked directly to the tree where these men were seated. Little did I know that from that moment on my life would change forever. I didn't even continue on with my stroll. I was close enough now that the voice was saying words that I understood—music, singing. I listened as the voice was telling the group about a place back in the hills where they played music and sung songs every day, a place called Renfro Valley. I listened to the conversation, and as soon as the group began to disperse, I walked up to this gentlemen, stuck out my hand and introduced myself. I told him that I was also in hillbilly music, and I kept asking questions until he asked me if I would like to be a guest on the Renfro Valley show, the *Renfro Valley Barn Dance*. He told me guest acts were a regular part of the performance every Saturday night and that he would set it up with the boss man, a John Lair. He told me he sang bass in a gospel quartet that was a regular feature of the *Barn Dance*.

When I got back home a couple of days later I told my buddy about the contact that I had made and immediately we made plans to head up to Renfro Valley the following Saturday. We found it on the map 250 miles away, a long piece in that day and time. I had bought a 1941 Studebaker, and this is the reason the show was already under way when we arrived. I remember we pulled into the parking lot out in front of the Old Barn and got into a sort of a heated discussion about which one was going to go in to let them know that we were there and explain why we were late. Well, in spite of that, everything went great. We were a hit! John Lair wasn't in the Valley that night; he was in New York, and for that reason we were invited back.

Two weeks later we returned to the *Renfro Valley Barn Dance* for another guest appearance, and once again John Lair was away on business. In addition to making a hit with the audience, we hit it off

Pete Stamper and Clarence Williams in their roles as Clarence and Waldo.

with John Lair's sister, Puss (whose real name was Clyde), who attended every *Barn Dance* performance, watching the show from a front-row seat. On our second trip, she sent word backstage that John Lair had heard about our act and that if we wanted a job, come see him whenever we could. Fifteen months later, January 1952, we were able to come back for another guest appearance. This time Mr. Lair was there and put us on the payroll. That one split-second on an August afternoon at Fort Campbell, Kentucky, when time for me stood still just long enough for me to change the direction I was headed, changed every aspect of my life from that moment on.

Renfro Valley's format was such that an inexperienced entertainer had the opportunity to learn and grow. I made the acquaintance of a local boy, Lee Earl Hysinger, who later introduced me to Minnie Lee Taylor, the girl who would become my wife. At Renfro Valley I met and worked with Betty Foley, who later introduced me to her father, Red Foley, who invited me to join him in America's first network TV country music show, *The Ozark Jubilee*, where I met and worked with Porter Wagoner, who later introduced me to Dolly Parton. Yes, all because of a moment in time on a hot August afternoon in 1950.

I've never looked back to that moment with regret in the least. I've made a number of decisions since that time that I maybe would change if I could, but not that one, no, never. I have wondered if maybe there might have been more than a spark of curiosity that turned me aside, more than just the fickle hand of fate, more than just good luck. Maybe the good Lord had a hand in my direction. The only decision that I had ever made that was more important than this one was the one I made for him a few years earlier.

Wouldn't the Lord be concerned about where a young Christian worked and played? Oh, but there was more to it than that, since my life was not the only one changed by that moment. Remember, I had a partner, Clarence Ray Williams. We were a team, a comedy team, the comedy team of Clarence and Waldo, and we were good, if I have to say so myself. We were not the musicians Homer & Jethro were, but our material was fresh and funny and our songwriting talents were clicking. There was a bright future up ahead of us, and we knew we had the talents to make it happen. But there was a problem. My partner's friendship with the bottle came between him and his performance. After such a short while in Renfro Valley, we went our separate ways. I went home first, then received word from John Lair that he thought I might be able to work alone. I returned to Renfro Valley.

Clarence had met a musician from Chicago who invited him to accompany him to the Windy City. There he went to work in one of the Mafia-owned and -operated nightclubs on Chicago's south side, a place that owns you lock, stock, and barrel, a place that held his guitar behind locked doors to keep him from leaving until they were ready for him to go. One night, a slow night, the musicians were playing to a small house. One of the strippers who worked there came around to the bandstand and asked my buddy, Smiley, as he was called then, to sing a special song for her, but Smiley refused and explained why he couldn't. She demanded that he sing the song, and again he refused and explained why he could not. She threw such a fit, made such a commotion, it attracted the attention of the boss, who just happened to be the stripper's boyfriend and also a hitman for the Mafia family who ran that side of Chicago. When she told him that Smiley wouldn't sing her song, he, too, wanted to know why. Smiley explained that she wanted to hear "The Old Rugged Cross" and that he couldn't sing that song in a place like that. The boss let him know that what he wanted or didn't want didn't count in a place like that. He said, "You sing her song." And once again Smiley said, "I can't do it. I won't do it." The man reached under his coat, came out with a pistol and placed it between Smiley's eyes and said, "You will sing 'The Old Rugged Cross' or I will blow your head off." Smiley said he knew that the man was a man of his word if nothing else, but he said he decided then and there that he would rather die for having refused to sing it than to live after having done it. And just when he thought that was it, the stripper said, "Oh, forget it. I didn't want to hear the song anyway."

From Chicago's south side, Clarence's next stop was Skid Row in Evansville, Indiana. Here, according to his own admission, his life sank so low that he had to be helped up to his knees. But on his knees he found the way back to standing tall. For the past thirty years or so, Reverend Clarence Williams has established and pastored a number of churches in Indiana and North Carolina. He and his wife, Mary, have written songs recorded by some of the well-known gospel groups, and his son, Hank Williams, is a full-time evangelist holding crusades throughout the country. Reverend Clarence Williams and family are always comfortable with their visits to Renfro Valley, where "The Old Rugged Cross" is sung quite often. So you can see why I am comfortable with giving the good Lord my thanks for turning me toward the man with the voice, the deep bass voice that stopped me in my tracks and changed my life forever, the voice of the late Reverend Morris M. Gaskins.

While I was away in Springfield, Missouri, as a part of Red's TV show, the television cameras were rolling in Renfro Valley. Mr. Lair and the Folks did a series of programs that were first class in every respect. I believe they were formatted similar to the Monday night Bugler Tobacco programs he did on radio in the early forties. That format has proven itself, for with a few minor changes here and there it became the *Sunday Morning Gatherin'*. This might have been the break the Valley needed, but doing a show like this on location was just too expensive. It is even today, so you can just imagine how it must have been in 1956. I have heard some of the entertainers talk about how, while the production company and camera crews sat around, Mr. Lair would be off in his office writing his scripts just as if time really was standing still. To go to a studio to shoot a Renfro

Granny Harper and Slim Miller, 1949.

Valley show would not even be considered. He would do it at Renfro Valley or not at all. I helped to close out the fifties; but 1958 and 1959 were years I would just as soon forget.

I returned to Renfro Valley after an absence of almost four years, and I wasn't ready for the changes that had taken place. I had thought coming back to Renfro Valley was a smart move on my part. I had been living in Nashville, hoping to become a member of the Grand Ole Opry. Rod Brasfield, comedian for the Opry, was having some

TV comes to Renfro Valley. Shooting a scene in John Lair's office for one of thirteen TV shows made in 1956. (Note the size of the camera equipment.)

health problems at the time, and I was working off and on in his place on the NBC Prince Albert portion. I was doing road shows with Porter Wagoner about the same time that rock 'n roll music was putting the finishing touches to the damage television had put on country music concerts. No one was making a killin'. Porter wasn't working all that much and was only able to pay me about half of what I was making when we were working together in Springfield. I had a little family to take care of, and I just wasn't making enough money to survive for a long period of time in a high cost of living area like Nashville. I reasoned that I could do everything I was then doing by moving back to Renfro Valley and commuting to Nashville. That's when I learned the lesson of "Out of sight, out of mind." But that's another story.

Mr. Lair wanted me back in Renfro Valley and convinced me that I was just exactly what his little, new 500-watt radio station needed.

Old Joe Clark was becoming a star all over again, at least for a radius of thirty-five miles in all directions on a clear day. If I could do just half as well as Old Joe was doing, everything was going to work out fine. I lasted all of six months before the manager, Tom Hargis, had to tell me that it just wasn't working out. I was just one of those who failed as a disc jockey; Slim Miller and Claud Sweet both had bit the dust in short order. I'd make a comeback at WRVK later, but I needed a job right then. We all needed a job right then because the *Barn Dance* and the *Gatherin'*, though still on the air, were without sponsors. That meant for the first time in the twenty-year history of Renfro Valley there was no money coming in, except from the ticket sales at the *Barn Dance*. For the first time Renfro Valley was not able to support its entertainers, and the entertainers could no longer support themselves through personal appearances. Many of the *Barn Dance* and *Gatherin'* talent with whom I had worked had already gone by the time I got back, and those who were still there were trying to leave.

As I mentioned, Slim Miller was still around, but his health had begun to fail and he was missing more and more of the shows. Slim wasn't too happy to see me come back, I don't suppose. I didn't find out until not too long ago that Slim really didn't like me too much. Joe Clark just recently broke that news to me, but I always knew that he wasn't too friendly toward me. I hope it was just because I was competition to him and for no other reason than that.

I remember back when I first came to Renfro Valley in 1952, I had been around there for six months, just working the *Barn Dance,* doing nothing else, needing money, needing work real bad. Slim came around to me one day and suggested that he might have a booking he could use me on and wondered if I was interested in going. Naturally, I told him I was, then he got around to asking me if he could borrow my spare tire to make the trip. I could have just as easily given him all five tires because I wasn't making enough money to drive my car. And I remember him telling me we would go on a certain day at 11:30. Plans were for them to pick me up at my cabin. Well, the night before we were to leave I wrote the folks back home telling them what I'd been doing and what I was going to do the next day; I'd be making my first personal appearance with the Renfro Valley Folks. I'd be going into a state I'd never been in before, the big state of Ohio, and when I finished my letter, I went to bed, set my alarm for 9:00 the next morning and was ready to go at 10:00 A.M. I sat around for an hour and a half. Eleven thirty came; eleven thirty went. And no Renfro Valley

Folks. I waited until 12:00 or 12:30, still no one. Finally I ventured outside, and I happened to run into someone who informed me that Slim and gang had left out at daylight that morning. My spare tire made the trip to Ohio, but Waldo stayed home. I was to learn many times in the years to come that "That's Show Business!"

The Coon Creek Girls closed out the year 1957 still with the *Barn Dance* and the *Gatherin'*. But they had already made up their minds to disband and call it quits, something that they would do in just a matter of days. Black-eyed Susie was working at a variety of jobs in the Valley. She was music librarian and helped put out our *Bugle* newspaper each month, a job that she had held since its beginning in 1943. She would continue on as a part-time harmony singer, filling in as bass player on the *Barn Dance* and the *Gatherin'*. She was now getting married to WRVK engineer Jack Jennings, and this union would soon take her out of the Valley for good. Lily May and husband, Glen Pennington, would continue to make their home in the Renfro Valley area, as would Rosey and Cotton Foley.

Two or three years earlier, Glen had become a partner in a Ford automobile dealership with Cotton. This move on Glen's part would help him to accumulate the capital to become one of the future owners of Renfro Valley. He once told me how he first discovered he could sell. When he was a member of a gospel quartet in Knoxville, Tennessee, they were working at a radio station and their program was sponsored by an automobile dealer. One Saturday, as a promotional gimmick to bring attention to the business and the radio program, they announced that the members of the quartet would be on the lot that Saturday and would be competing with the regular sales force. Glenn outsold all the quartet members and even beat out most of the experienced car salesmen. And he said he never forgot that. He was not only a good salesman, he was a good businessman. He had a knack for knowing how to mix business with pleasure.

I well remember in 1957 when I came back to Berea, Kentucky, with a prestigious show to take part in the annual Berea homecoming. Red Foley was the star along with Pat Boone and Jimmie Skinner, the Foggy River Boys, Betty Foley, and others. The car dealers in Madison county were furnishing convertibles for the parade that day, and Glen Pennington furnished the one that I rode in. Had my name on the side and everything. I had just bought me a new 8mm movie camera for the occasion. I brought it along and took pictures of Pat and Red and everyone else in the show. We paraded to one end of the town, turned and came back to the other end, where Glen Pennington's automobile business was located. Glen pulled into the lot there, and he said, "Say, you know, you'll want to be on that film. Step outside the car here, get up there where we can see your name. Give me that camera and wave and smile." And I did exactly as he said. I stood out by the car and I waved, and shouted, and smiled, and everything, and he pointed the camera, and pushed the button, and shot and shot, and wound and shot again. And I felt so proud and so important. Here I was, being photographed by the one who just three years earlier was teaching me this hillbilly music business.

I was back home in Springfield, Missouri, about three weeks later when the film came back from the developers, and I hurriedly put it on the projector and sat back to watch the parade, especially that part at the end where I would be waving hello and showing off alongside my own personalized parade car. I got one quick half a second glimpse at what I had been expecting to see. Glen raised the camera just enough above my head to get the letters of the big red and blue sign that read "Foley-Pennington Ford," and that's all you could see for the next couple of minutes. Boy, if that wasn't enough to take the wind out of your sails and bring your head down to size! I mentioned that to him a few years later, in 1989 when once again he became my boss. Glen grinned and said, "Say, I'd like to see that sometime." But he never did.

Dick Dickerson, Renfro Valley's hot steel guitar player, had left the Valley for a job at a Lexington radio station. He would drop back in to say hello now and then. Wayne Turner, the smoothest voice in Renfro Valley or on any other show, had already left the Valley when I returned. In 1957, Wayne stopped in to say hello on his way through to his home in Arizona. I never knew his whereabouts after that. Ray Sosby was no longer bringing his fiddle down from Ohio on the weekends. Roy Davidson was still working both the *Barn Dance* and the *Gatherin'*, but he had gone to work in Ohio with the Crosley Company and was commuting on weekends and would for a few more years. Junior Defore was no longer making his weekend trips up from Georgia, as he had done for so many years. I believe Jerry Behrens was still on the program for just a few weeks but decided that he would give the printing business a try. He moved his family to Mt. Vernon and set up a print shop, or at least that was his plan. Jerry was in and out of the Valley more than anyone I knew. A time or two he would move his family all the way back to his home in Louisiana for a few years, then back to the Valley he would come. His last visit was in 1993. He was an old man, feeble in body and mind, but he made another trip to Renfro Valley. We paid a lot of attention to Jerry, acknowledging the fact that he was in the audience that night. We invited him to our autograph session, folks came through, he autographed their souvenir books, they talked to Jerry. I shook hands with him, told him I hoped to see him again sometime. He said, "The next time you see me, I'll be back here in Renfro Valley." While Jerry never was able to return before his death, which soon followed, he kept for a while his dream of coming back home to Renfro Valley.

One-armed banjo player Emory Martin and his pretty wife, Linda Lou, had said good-bye to the stage and had settled in the shadows of the Old Barn. Emory and his brother, Curtis, rented the Renfro Valley Gulf service station from Mr. Lair. By the way, that's the building that now houses our ticket office. Linda Lou had gone to work at the Rockcastle County Hospital. Now, this Gulf service station under Emory's management was a godsend for me. I had come back to Renfro Valley driving a brand spankin' new yellow and black Ford Fairlane 500 hardtop with a continental kit and dragging a lien as long as your leg. I had never owed so much on a car. Never in my life had I let a car go back, but I couldn't afford to keep this one without a job.

I went to Ohio one weekend with a friend of mine, Lee Earl Hysinger. He needed to borrow a car from his cousin, Rube Anglin, who was in the automobile business in Hamilton, Ohio. And while I was there I asked Rube if he could take my car off my hands and give me one that I wouldn't owe any money on. Well, he considered this every way, right and left, top and bottom, and decided that he just did not have anything on the lot that he could afford to make that kind of a trade with. But he did say he was about to trade for one that afternoon that I might have. And, sure enough, before we left there that day, the trade was made and I went away with a 1951 red Studebaker that had been around the world a time or two.

That car became a permanent fixture in Emory Martin's garage. It was usually some little something minor that I could fix myself, and they would just let me use the rack free of charge. Of course, after I started working on it, Emory would always come 'round and lend me a hand. He would have loaned me two if he'd had them. He is that kind of a fella. I finally took the car back to Anglin's Auto Sales and traded it for a Kaiser. These two cars plus one or two others we owned over the years finally led to my writing a song that resulted in my first recording in 1959 with Dot Records called "A Cheva-Kaiser-Olds-Mo-Laca-Stud-War-Linco-Baker."

When Claud Sweet didn't make it as a disc jockey, he leased the Scenic View Motel just a mile north of Renfro Valley, now a part of the Family Life Center. This kept Claud around the Valley for a little while, but soon he, too, went to Ohio, where he took a job in a factory, quitting the *Barn Dance* and entertaining in the clubs a little closer to his new home. Claud Sweet was Mr. Personality Plus on the *Barn Dance*. As far as I am concerned, he had the most friendly smile that I'd ever seen on anyone. I could watch him sing a country, boogie, blues, or gospel song and get the feeling Claud was living every word. As much as Mr. Lair disliked rock music, and he felt strong about it, he gave the okay for Claud to do a number or two by Little Richard and Jerry Lee Lewis that were on the charts. Claud was best known for a thing called "Flamin' Mamie, That High Geared Mama." It wasn't rock, but it was hot. Like Elvis, he moved. I don't mean the way Elvis moved, but he just had a happy movement, a rhythm about him. He even moved when he talked to you. Fact of the matter is, a fella that played a part in Elvis's early career saw Claud one time and offered to take him under his wing and give him a try. After thinkin' about it awhile, Claud decided not to make the change, a decision that he would express regrets about many times in his later years.

Rhuel and Flossie Thomas of the Crusaders and the 76 Gospel Quartets had left entertainment and settled down to their farm and feed business. For a good many years Rhuel was John Lair's right-hand man. When Mr. Lair had to be away from the Valley, Rhuel helped with the emcee work on the *Barn Dance* and narrated the *Sunday Morning Gatherin'*. I understand he made a little money available to Mr. Lair a time or two in the winters when the going was rough. Rhuel and Flossie left the shows before I made it back to Renfro Valley, but, before they did, they introduced the Valley to three young school-teachers and gospel singers also from Clinton County who would have a strong influence on the Valley for the next twenty-five years.

As far as service to the Valley was concerned Bess, Marie, and Hazel Farmer would equal or surpass the Coon Creek Girls. They would establish themselves as permanent fixtures in all activities in and out of the Valley. Bess played the accordion on the Saturday night *Barn Dance* and Ma Lair's old parlor organ on the *Sunday Morning Gatherin'*. Marie did the talking for all three. She did enough talking for six, and

The Coon Creek Girls in 1952: Lily May, Rosey, and Black-eyed Susie.

Hazel and Bess would just smile and be a little embarrassed at some of the things that Marie had to say. The Farmer Sisters' talents fit the *Gatherin'* to a T, and their personalities made for a fun-loving Saturday night *Barn Dance*. I included Marie in my comedy act from time to time, and when I would choose one of the other girls on the show, Marie would threaten me with the police. She would say, "You leave me out one more time, and the police are going to be watching your car. You speed one mile over the speed limit and they are going to be after you." She was talking about Hazel's new husband, a fella who originally came from my hometown down in western Kentucky named

The Farmer Sisters: Hazel, Bess, and Marie.

Willis Martin who stood about 6 foot 6 or 7 or 8 and was a member of the Kentucky State Police.

One time the Farmers and I played a show up in Michigan, a state fair up there. We had a little time to spare when we got in, so Marie wanted to go out on the fairgrounds and do a little riding. She picked a contraption there that whupped you around, stirred you up, and jerked you this way and that way. She didn't have any luck with Bess, but she did talk Hazel and me into getting on this thing with her. She got on first, Hazel got on next, and then I got on the other side. The very first round this thing made, Hazel ended up halfway in my lap, her arms around my neck, screaming her head off. Calm, cool, and collected as you'd want to be, Marie was over with her Instamatic camera taking pictures. Had either Willis or my wife been watching this, they'd a thought nothing of it, but when those pictures came back, it looked like "a hot time in the old town tonight." Marie blackmailed her way in on my act for quite a long time. It was all in fun, I think.

While the professional entertainers were having to take outside jobs for the first time or at least the first time in many years, the new talent that was, as they say, "coming on board," were folks who had always held jobs but had never entertained professionally. For that reason, most of them were the home-grown variety—that is, from Rockcastle and surrounding counties. In place of the Coon Creek Girls, there were now two all-girl groups in addition to the Farmer Sisters. From over in the Berea area came the talented Begley Sisters. These young ladies were straight off the farm in Madison County. And from Rockcastle County, it was the Bullock Sisters—Arlene, Gwen and Jerri. They were becoming mighty popular with the Saturday night *Barn Dance* crowd. A younger sister, ten-year-old Linda, was winning talent contests around the county, and she would take her place along with Kathy Brown when Arlene and Jerri decided to pursue other interests. The Bullock Sisters were a part of our *Renfro Valley Barn Dance* for close to fifteen years.

Don Harper, another Rockcastle County product, was a watch tinker in Mt. Vernon when he first brought his guitar out for an audition with Mr. Lair. I read someplace where Mr. Lair wrote that when he first heard Don play, he thought to himself, "Well, here's a good farm hand going to waste." But I guess Don had improved a lot because the next time he auditioned, he was hired. Mr. Lair would later say that Don was one of the three best guitar players that he had ever had working for him.

More and more, Slim Miller was spending time in the hospital or away from the show recuperating. Mr. Lair latched on to a fiddle player from nearby Garrard County. Most of the fiddling he'd been doing was at square dances around the country and, specifically, just up the road about seven miles in Brodhead at the fairgrounds' Square Dance

Barn. Fiddling was fun for Bee Lucas. When he went to work it was as a body man at a Ford garage in Lancaster, Kentucky. To listen to Bee fiddle on a Saturday night or on the *Sunday Morning Gatherin'*, it was hard to believe that just a few hours earlier, those same hands were banging the dents out of automobile fenders. As I write, Bee is in a nursing home out in the state of Kansas. He doesn't remember much about Renfro Valley now, if anything at all, but we have fond memories of him. His sense of humor and the practical jokes I remember most of all.

I recall one Sunday morning after the *Gatherin'* when most everyone had gone over to the Lodge for breakfast. Some of us hung around the radio station. Marie Farmer had left her car parked out in the parking lot, and someone caught a black snake that ended up in Marie's automobile. It was supposed to be in the front seat when Marie came back to get in her car, but no one told the snake. It found its way in, down and around, and up and behind the upholstery. Now, no one was going to let Marie drive away with a snake hidden in her car, so naturally someone told her, and Marie took this little practical joke just about the way you would have expected her to. After she calmed down and put her thinking cap on, Marie said, "Somebody go find Bee Lucas—he'll know what to do." We brought Bee around, and she offered to pay him if he would go into the car, take part of the upholstery off, and get the snake out, which he did. After all, here was an experienced body man. He could have been an experienced poker player, because he did all this work, took the money, thanked her, and let her go on her way. Marie didn't find out until a couple of years ago when I let the cat out of the bag in one of my *Bugle* articles that it was Bee who put the snake in there in the first place.

About that time there was a young man from over in Jackson county, a schoolteacher by trade, with so many interests that paralleled those of John Lair that the two were bound to meet somewhere along the line. Ralph Marcum had that pioneer spirit. He felt at home in a bearskin coat and a coonskin cap, and he knew how to make, as well as fire, those old flintlock rifles. I don't think I ever heard what brought him to the Valley in the first place, but something brought him face to face with John Lair. Mr. Lair mentioned that he thought he looked like a fiddle player, and he told Ralph that if he ever learned to play the fiddle to come back and see him sometime. Now, I do know that he was running a little bit short on fiddle players, but this might have just been a nice way of sending a young man on his way in good spirits. He might never have expected to see him again. However, that encouragement was all little Ralph Marcum needed. He went home, made arrangements to get that first fiddle, and, before a year was up, Ralph was back in the Valley. He had learned two fiddle tunes, and one of them he played for John Lair and played it good enough to get a spot on the show. He would claim that spot on Saturday nights over the next thirty years. Many of a Saturday night he'd bring that Old Barn to life with his lightening-fast version of the "Orange Blossom Special," but if Ralph ever learned anything other than those two numbers, I never knew it.

John Lair never did cotton to the philosophy "If you can't beat em, join em," but he didn't mind tinkering just a little bit with the fads of the day as long as he could control 'em. He set out to build his own teen idol from the makin's of a young man from over in the Jackson County area by the name of Boyd Ingram. There really wasn't a lot of makin' over to be done. Boyd was as handsome as a young fella dared to be, blond locks of hair and an easy-going, quiet personality to go along with it. It wasn't until we made our movie in 1965 that Mr. Lair went all out and hired some young girls to sit in the audience and scream when Boyd came on. He teamed Boyd with Ann Honeycutt for the love angle of the movie. Ann was a pretty young lady who worked with the Farmer Sisters from time to time.

WRVK

In April 1957, Renfro Valley's little radio station, WRVK, made its debut on the air. It came on with the fanfare fitting of a 50,000 watter. Tom Hargis, Mr. Lair's partner in this venture, was fresh out of Hollywood. The two of them had worked together at WLS in Chicago, where Tom had also met Gene Autry. His years in Hollywood were spent as producer, director, and editor of western radio shows for Gene Autry, Roy Rogers, and other cowboy stars. Hollywood actors and actresses had recorded messages of good wishes for broadcast on that opening day, along with recordings and telegrams from dignitaries from the political and country music world. Hundreds of folks showed up in person for the fun, food, and music.

For Tom Hargis, WRVK was most likely a retirement investment since television had had the same effect on radio westerns as it had had on country music. But I always believed that the real reason John Lair wanted his own radio station was because it was radio that let him have Renfro Valley in the first place. Whatever the reason, WRVK would be the most important addition that would be made to Renfro Valley for many a year. In spite of the fact that Mr. Lair knew so much about the entertainment side of the microphone, he knew practically nothing about the business side of radio, a fact that he would prove later when he literally gave his little station away.

I can tell you of another example of when "what John said" and "what John did" were two different things. I remember reading two editorials in our *Renfro Valley Bugle*. One dealt with the format of radio changing from live entertainment to recorded music; the other dealt with rock 'n roll of the day, both of which John disapproved. The article concerning recorded music even suggested that the people, the listeners, were to blame for not rising up and demanding that the stations go back to live entertainment. In the other editorial he blamed rock 'n roll music for all the meanness that was going on around the country. While he was writing these editorials, at the very same time on his own little radio station there was very little live music; most of it was recordings from daylight to dark. And one of the most popular shows on the station was an afternoon rock 'n roll show.

The disk jockey handling this program was Russ Fisher. Russ and his wife, Jo Nell, had moved to Renfro Valley the very day WRVK went on the air. They had been driving the 200 miles each weekend from Russellville, Kentucky, to perform on the *Barn Dance* and the *Sunday Morning Gatherin'*. They were a sweetheart vocal team. Russ was lead guitar player and Jo Nell played rhythm guitar. They were a big asset to Renfro Valley in many ways. Russ took to disc jockeying like a duck takes to water; however, he was a most unlikely rock jockey. Russ was middle-aged, he was bald, yet Russ had a talent for communicating with the teenagers that most of us didn't have. Russ pretty much became the anchor for WRVK for a while, doing the news programs and, most important, acting as straight man for Old Joe Clark both on radio and on stage. He also became John Lair's right-hand man, taking up where Rhuel Thomas had left off some time before. Russ would emcee some of the *Barn Dance* shows and take care of the *Gatherin'* in Mr. Lair's absence. Jo Nell would come to play the most important role of any individual on the *Sunday Morning Gatherin'*, except, of course, John Lair himself. She played rhythm in the *Gatherin'* band, sang duets with her husband, sang in the girls' trio, and her solo vocals held a featured spot for many years. After Russ died, she became Mrs. Kit Simunick, married to a man who had fallen in love with that Renfro Valley Sunday morning voice many years earlier.

The *Renfro Valley Barn Dance* and the *Gatherin'* indirectly benefitted from WRVK, as it was the radio station that kept three or four of us entertainers around the Valley for a good many years when otherwise we more than likely would have had to move on. In fact, when I ended my association with the station in its thirtieth year, I had spent twenty-two years as one of its disc jockeys or as station manager. And I found that the guests who attended the *Barn Dance* and the *Gatherin'* really expected Renfro Valley to have a radio station. They made some connection between their station at home and the

Russ and Jo Nell Fisher.

one that they found in the Valley. There was really no connection, as WRVK was mostly just a local business. But WRVK inherited the broadcast studios and the big, log museum building that had been built for the daily radio shows and the *Gatherin'* when they were broadcast on WHAS and CBS. Few stations of any size had as nice a home. Its main, or big studio, as it was called, is all decked out with oil portraits of some of the pioneers of early radio folk music, but most fascinating is the upper border of the room, where there is a mural depicting folk music from its stone age on through to the present day. In fact, the last part of the painting shows the Renfro Valley Folks in that very same studio at work at the microphone. So it was easy for visitors to the Valley to suppose that the programs that they were hearing back home were still coming straight from that room. "What was still is," since you see the room, all the paintings intact, now used as a part of the John Lair Dining Room and sought after by small groups.

WRVK was born just about the time WHAS and CBS were giving up their ties to Renfro Valley. We no longer had a national audience to entertain, but we kept busy taking our Rockcastle County listeners to the county fairs and the tobacco festivals. We even broadcast from the homes of some of the listeners. One of our sponsors was a flour company that sent our announcers into the kitchens of some of our listeners to get favorable testimony about their product direct from the cooks. There were times they didn't get the favorable comments they were after.

Long before there were More For Less or Save-A-Lot grocery stores, there was Caleb Sowder's. This was a grocery store in a big, old rundown building out in the country about three or four miles out of town. And that's where WRVK would plug in its remote microphone every Friday morning for a live broadcast and sometimes live music along with records, of course, and the grocery specials of the week. Caleb's, and later Clayton's, as it was known, would do a business that would be the envy of any supermarket chain. If Old Joe Clark said it was good or good for you, people bought it sight unseen or taste untested. Old Joe Clark and WRVK were sort of like radio and Renfro Valley; they just went together.

Tom Hargis had made available to the little station one of the finest sound effects libraries ever made, one that he had used when he was a producer of Hollywood shows. And Old Joe Clark made use of it. He had freight trains running through the studios, milk cows, and mule teams. Folks up and down the hollers around really got into Old Joe and his early morning madness. Once he pretended he was building a moonshine still, and each day he would add just a little bit more, a little bit more, a little bit more. Friday morning came....He fired her up and—BOOM—it blew up! In every home up and down the hollers and around, parts of that still fell for five minutes. One feller even got so caught up in it he drove out to the station to see for himself.

Joe Clark on the radio.

Now, regardless of how Old Joe Clark came across on the air, Joe was really not at home at the control board. He was a little up-tight and nervous if anything went wrong. For this reason, every now and then some of us would make sure that things would go wrong for Old Joe. After turning on the transmitter in the morning, the first "on the air" function that he did was to play the national anthem. You couldn't mistake the cart (cartridge, or cassette, we call them now) that played the national anthem. Not only did it have the words "National Anthem" written on it but someone had drawn stars and stripes down the side, so it was second nature for Joe to pick up the right cart, insert it in the machine, and push the button that would play the national anthem. Now, when that button was pushed, you would hear the big band sound of the national anthem coming from over in the corner speaker in the studio with you. This is what you expected to hear; this is what you did hear; this is what Joe heard morning after morning after morning, week after week after week, year after year. You just didn't expect anything else.

Well, one night I was working late at the station and I was thinking about all this taking place the next morning, so I recorded the national anthem on another cart. But ahead of the national anthem, I yelled, "Good Morning, Joe!" just like Robin Williams would later yell, "Good Morning, Vietnam!" So Joe wouldn't suspect anything, I took the label off the original cart and placed it on my counterfeit, placed it back where Joe would expect to find it, went home, and set my alarm for early in the morning so I'd be able to listen.

Sure enough, the next morning I could tell that the transmitter had been turned on, and I sat there waiting. Suddenly I heard, "Good Morning, Joe!" But that's all I heard; the national anthem didn't play then as I had thought it would. Joe Clark must have been lightning fast that morning to push that stop button. Not knowing the national anthem was on that tape, but mainly not knowing what else I was going to say, Joe refused to push any more buttons. Fact of the matter is, the joke ended up on me. I had to get up and go down to the station and help him find the national anthem so he could get on the air in the correct manner.

Like I said, I could write a book about Old Joe Clark and WRVK. In the days we're talking about, we thought of the FCC (the Federal Communications Commission) as kind of like the Gestapo. They would show up when you least expected them; they would start checking equipment, read your reports; they never dared to smile; they wouldn't act friendly in any shape, form or fashion. Old Joe knew about the FCC, but he had paid more attention to Tom Hargis and the engineer's insistence that no one was allowed in that control room—absolutely no one but the man who was on duty. No one for any reason whatsoever!

There were two small rooms that separated the control room from the front door, and each one had a lock. The front door was unlocked. If you wanted to talk to the man on duty, you came into the first little room, pushed a button to get his attention, and then you were permitted to talk to him through about a five-inch by ten-inch hole in the wall. There was another entrance behind the disc jockey in a hall a few feet away that stayed locked, only used by the employees of the station. Now, it was this entrance that the FCC man found open the morning that he showed up on Old Joe Clark's tour of duty. And, I suppose, just as he had done at hundreds and hundreds of stations all around the nation, he walked down the hall until he found the studio and, unannounced, he walked in behind Old Joe, reached up and took the log down from off the wall and started twisting the knobs on the transmitter. Well, Old Joe became aware of his presence, wheeled around and yelled, "What in the blankety-blank do you think you're doing?" He tells Old Joe he's the FCC. Joe says, "I don't care who in the blankety-blank you are, you touch another one of them knobs and I am going to break your blankety-blank arm. Now get the blankety-blank out of here!" Joe put him outside and locked the front door, and that's where the man stayed until Tom Hargis showed up about 9:00. Tom said, "I'm the manager." The man says, "I'm the FCC. What I want to know is who in the blankety-blank you got in there."

WRVK had a number of engineers over the years. First, I believe, was Jack Jennings. Then came Ted Foster, who made his way to WRVK out of the state of Texas; Hal Whatley, Old Joe Clark's flower-peddling buddy; and Tiny (I don't recall Tiny's given name). There was also Arvil Jones and Maurice Lackey.

One of the big sponsors at WRVK was a company that made Silver Mist Flour. They promoted their product by going into the homes of the radio listeners and giving cash awards to any lady who could show that she had Silver Mist on her cabinet shelf. Old Joe and engineer Hal Whatley, with remote equipment, microphones, and flour samples under their arms, would go from door to door out in the boondocks of Rockcastle and surrounding counties recording their interviews with the lady of the house for broadcast the following day. You would have to hear Old Joe tell it to know just what he went through on this job and how bad he hated it. I'd tell you like he told me but we might get an X rating from the publisher. He has told of being bitten by dogs, chased by turkey gobblers, and about one woman who threatened to shoot them both if they didn't get off of her kitchen porch. To show the lady they meant no harm, Hal handed her a couple of sacks of flour, which she immediately threw at them as they scurried back to the safety of their automobile.

And there was Tiny. As I said, I don't recall Tiny's name, but Larry Burdette, present owner of WRVK, met Tiny at Fanfare in Nashville one year and learned that he was a radio engineer, disk jockey, and sales person. Well, Larry was manager of the station at the time and was looking for a way to promote and increase the sale of WRVK. Tiny weighed in at around 400 pounds. He more than filled every compartment of the specially made overalls and bright plaid shirt that he was wearing when Larry met him. It just so happened that the station needed an engineer and disk jockey, so Larry invited him up and promised him a job. Larry came home telling about this wonderful find that he'd made. He said, "What a novelty. The county would go wild over Tiny." Well, about Tuesday of the following week, a big long Cadillac eased off the highway with the passenger side riding up in the air about a foot higher than the driver's side, parked in front of the station, and out stepped the biggest woman I have ever seen. Well, not really a woman, but a man in a woman's dress. Tiny, with his engineering tools, made his way into the station and was ready to go to work. Well, Larry almost had a heart attack. He came into the station later in the day, and there sat Tiny in his long granny dress working on microphone cables. When Larry approached him about his unusual costume, he simply told Larry that he liked to be comfortable. That was all that he wore during the months he was here in the Valley. As far as I know, he was a fine engineer, and I will have to agree, he *was* the talk of the county!

I guess I was better acquainted with Arvil Jones than anyone else of the engineering staff. Arvil was a workaholic. In addition to his duties as an engineer at two or three radio stations, he had a number of other projects either in the works or in the planning stage. I don't recall if he was in the TV repair business or if he was just doing Old Joe Clark a favor, but I remember him taking a TV that belonged to Old Joe Clark to see if he could remedy a very rare problem. Somehow Old Joe had spilled a quart of molasses down inside his television. I asked him once how this happened, and he wouldn't tell me. He said I wouldn't believe him anyway. Well, it seems that Arvil took the TV home with him and set it out on his back porch until he could find the time to figure out how he was going to fix it. That's where it sat for four or five weeks. When Arvil did get around to checking it out, he found that the ants had found it first and had eaten all the molasses right down to the last drop. Arvil hooked it up; it worked fine. Arvil brought it back to Old Joe and charged him $35 for cleaning it up. Joe was just about to fork over the money when Arvil told him about the help that he got from the ants. Joe just stuck $15 back in his pocket and told Arvil that was what he was charging him for feeding his ants for a month! I guess that's what you'd call TV dinners.

We had the cream of the crop in engineers, as I remember. They were to keep us on the air and to make sure that our signal was exactly at 1460 on the radio dial and as clean of interference as it could be. I recall soon after I went to work for the station in early 1958, a strange noise developed in the monitor at the studio. It was a low, rumbling noise. It was there, then it was gone, then it would return. I was new at this game, and I wasn't sure if it was something I should be concerned about or not. I had the early morning show and I was in the Valley all alone. Well, I should say I was in the station all alone, for in the Valley there was a house that sat about where Old Joe's restaurant is now located in our Village. This is where the station manager lived. Even though it wasn't time for him to come into the station office, I thought to be on the safe side I had better give him a call. I suppose knowing that I was inexperienced at operating a radio station, he maybe rushed over with more concern than he normally would have. After arriving, he listened to the noise that I had told him about and informed me that I had done the right thing in calling him. He began to check out the equipment but had no luck. He decided that the engineer had to be called. Now, the engineer had worked all night at the station and was home sleeping, which was the reason this decision was put off until the last minute. When the engineer arrived, he made a few checks here and there and finally decided the only way to solve this problem was to leave the air and go into it in a major way. He asked me to make the announcement on the air that, due to technical difficulties, we would be leaving the air and would return as soon as possible. In order for the engineer to get into the power supply, I had to remove all the records, the ash trays, and the other things that had accumulated there, including my coffee pot, and set them out in the floor. And he went to work. After going through the power supply from one end to the other, he said everything seemed to be in order. He began to put it back together, and soon we were back on the air. The monitor was as quiet as a mouse. Evidently he had solved the problem without really knowing what he had done. Soon he was replacing the records and the ashtrays and everything else back to the power supply console, including my coffeepot, which I plugged back in the wall, and in less than five minutes the monitor began to rumble again. Fortunately for me, the engineer had not gone back home to go to bed. When I called him in I told him about the noise and what I was doing when it came back and so forth, and he immediately zeroed in on my coffee pot. As that old pot would come on every few minutes to keep my coffee hot, somehow or other it managed to feed in on the monitor line. By the way, the name of my show was *Coffee Capers.*

The one piece of equipment our engineers were not authorized to work on was the Associated Press news machine that sat in a room isolated from the studio. It was just a sophisticated typewriter that sat typing night and day, day in and day out—that is, when it was not down for one reason or another. To get the Associated Press machine fixed when it needed it was a hassle, as the mechanic had to come all the way out of Corbin and sometimes Knoxville, Tennessee. On the day that President Kennedy was assassinated, I was driving toward Renfro Valley and had just left Berea city limits fifteen miles up the road when I got the news on my car radio. It was on all the stations up and down the dial, and I switched to 1460 to see what Old Joe Clark was having to say about it. My radio had buttons, and when one of them was pushed it set my dial smack dab on 1460, but there was no Old Joe Clark. In fact, there was no WRVK that I could tell. I wondered what had happened. I wondered if Joe Clark had left the air. But what about the voice I heard where WRVK should be? They were talking about the assassination all right, but it sure wasn't Joe. When I reached the station, I rushed in to find that Old Joe was holding the WRVK microphone up to the emergency broadcast system monitor that was set to receive a feed from WHAS in Louisville. Old Joe was rebroadcasting WHAS out over our signal. The Associated Press machine was down, and Joe was not receiving any news to broadcast of his own. Now, who says Old Joe Clark ain't got a head on him?

At the time this happened, Joe had been around the station a few years. His first experience with the Emergency Broadcast System is a story that's certainly worth telling. When the television show *WKRP in Cincinnati* first went on the air, I wondered if maybe the writers had been talking to someone who knew about the goings on at Renfro Valley's little WRVK. But as Jim Gaskin, Chubby Howard, and Don Gulley will tell you, all of them with broadcast experience, most little radio stations operate about the same. But only WRVK had Old Joe Clark. And I can't help but believe that set us apart from all the rest. Anyone who has spent any time at all around Old Joe knows full well talking comes as easy to him as breathing comes to most folks. But it has to come on his own terms. When you try to tell Joe what to say or when and how long to say it, look out for the results.

Trying to follow specific instructions, especially under pressure, when those instructions were not clearly defined in the first place, is another circumstance that brought on memorable results. The story might be called "Old Joe Clark and the Emergency Broadcast System." The EBS was the result of the frightening missile crisis in the early sixties. You know how it goes—"This is a test of the Emergency Broadcast System," followed by a few seconds of a high-pitched tone and then, "This has been a test of the Emergency Broadcast System. Had this been an actual emergency, you would have been informed where to tune for additional information. This concludes this test of the Emergency Broadcast System." When a special tone activated a gray boxlike receiver that sat on a shelf inside the WRVK control room, WRVK would receive the test from WHAS in Louisville. All we were to do was to enter the time the test was received onto the daily transmitter log and go about our business. Once a week at various times we were to send this test out over our own airwaves. But now, in addition to noting on the log, conducting a test required us to shut down the transmitter momentarily and then go back on the air for the conclusion of the test. Well, those tests were new, and no one was at ease with the responsibility of putting one of them on the air. I'm sure Old Joe lived dreading the day when it would come his time to take command. He for certain knew the seriousness of it all because the scare of the missile crisis had not worn off and, as I mentioned earlier, Old Joe had already had some dealing with the Federal Communications Commission. Then came one morning when there was no one around but Joe. That gray box came alive with the WHAS announcer saying, "This is a test of the Emergency Broadcast System." That's probably all Old Joe ever heard before his head kicked into emergency mode, and all the instructions he had absorbed over the past few weeks began to flood in on him. The action he took would have made even Barney Fife proud. I can't say that he announced a national emergency, but his listeners certainly had reason to wonder for a few minutes. In so many words Old Joe told them that the Emergency Broadcast System required him to leave the air for a time and if they wanted to know any more about what was going on they should tune in to WHAS in Louisville. He then proceeded to shut down the transmitter, turn off the lights, and lock the doors. He was found outside sitting on the steps waiting for who knows what when the engineer who was listening to the station from his sick bed at home came bounding out across the parking lot with a look of panic on his face. In spite of the confusion of the moment, the two were able to communicate enough information between them that the engineer learned the world was not coming to an end and Old Joe came to understand he had gone far beyond the call of duty. In a few minutes Joe was back on the air with his favorite Stanley Brothers music.

If I ever did write a book about WRVK I'd want to include my favorite memory. It was Christmas eve, and the last few strands of the national anthem were playing. The old clock on the wall was rolling up on 5:30 P.M. as I entered into the transmitter log the last reading for the day. In the next few seconds I would throw the switch that would put Renfro Valley's little 500-watt station to bed for the night. Suddenly the phone rang. It seemed like the phone was always ringing, but seldom at this hour. I picked up the receiver and answered, "WRVK." I was startled to hear a soft but cheerful voice say, "Goodnight, Pete." I was not surprised so much by what she said as I was by how quick she was gone. I hadn't even had time to return her greeting, much less learn her identity. I thought I had heard the voice someplace before, but I couldn't place it. I continued to relive the moment as I got back to doing the things you do at the close of a broadcast day. I wondered what she would be doing tomorrow and if she would call again. All I knew for sure was that all of a sudden I felt better. It gave me a warm feeling to know that she had been listening and had cared enough to call.

Old Joe Clark had headed down to Tennessee to visit kinfolk, so I would have all day Christmas Day to myself. I had only been working at the station for two months, so I thought it was important to take the holiday shift and establish myself as one of the team. I could have had help if I felt that I needed it. The station manager, Virginia Sutton, was good about filling in when needed. The engineer was someplace out there within listening distance and would have responded in an extreme emergency. But this day wasn't over for me just yet. All the station duties were wrapped up, but there was a little chore waiting for me out in the back studio closet. Santa Claus had left a few things that needed to be gift-wrapped and tagged with the names of my wife, Minnie Lee, my ten-year-old son, Jeff, my six-year-old daughter, Tracy, and my two-year-old son, Britt. Maybe in a couple of hours I could head home. I was still trying to figure out how I was going to be with the family when the presents were opened. Home was only three miles from the station, but that still didn't allow me to be in two places at once. Minnie Lee had suggested that maybe we could open the gifts on Christmas Eve, but this had never been the custom in our family, and I didn't want to spoil the surprise for the kids, even if it meant that I had to miss sharing it with them for once. This problem was solved about 4:30 A.M. Christmas morning when my son Jeff awoke to find Santa Claus had been there and proceeded to alert Tracy and Britt to the good news. We had our Christmas together after all.

After a quick breakfast and a cup of coffee, I headed out to spend the rest of the day with all of Rockcastle County—not really—not on Christmas Day. I knew our listening audience would probably be much smaller since family activities would keep some of them away, but I felt that the ones who were listening were counting on me to bring them their Christmas cheer. Renfro Valley was not a very cheerful place on that early Christmas morning. There were no lights on the tree. The Old Barn was empty and cold. Usually there would at least be someone in the post office, but this was Christmas and it was closed. Renfro Valley stood lonesome and dreary, but I would keep that to myself. Those who would visit me by way of the radio would have as bright a Christmas Day as I could make it for them. I had been setting aside a variety of holiday music and Christmas stories just for this occasion. The day went fast. I enjoyed selecting the programs I thought my listeners would enjoy. I enjoyed the many calls I received during the day wishing me and my family a Merry Christmas and a Happy New Year. I was tired but a little sorry to come to the end of that day. That was when I realized I had gotten so involved I hadn't thought about "my friend" since earlier that morning, but now it was all I did think about. Would she call again, and, if so, would I learn who she was? The national anthem had finished playing, and I realized I was standing in dead silence waiting. I reached to turn the transmitter off, once again thinking about her call the night before. I knew she was able to hear the moment the transmitter lost power, but the phone sat silent. I put my signature on the log and decided to call it a day. Just as my fingers touched the light switch, the phone rang. I jumped like I was shot. "WRVK," I said as I brought the receiver up to my ear. I heard in that same soft, smiling voice, "Goodnight, Pete." This time I said, "Goodnight," and together we hung up. For a few months after that, usually when I least expected it, she would call and tell me goodnight. She never told me who she was, and for some reason I never asked. That Christmas was many years ago. I have no reason to think she will ever see these words that I am writing today, but just in case, I would like to say once again, "Goodnight, whoever you are."

I'm amazed at how well John Lair handled his failures and disappointments. How he seemed to take them all in stride and go right on planning the future of Renfro Valley just as if everything was going to be all right up ahead. He had lost all of his radio sponsors and would in just a few weeks lose his *Barn Dance* broadcast altogether, a day that he had to know was coming. The CBS network would continue the *Gatherin'* until May of 1959 without a sponsor. He knew there was an end coming. The only good news came from the dozen stations that informed Mr. Lair that they would like to continue the *Gatherin'* if Renfro Valley would oblige by recording the show.

But before that happened, John tried a few tricks of his own. He would try Florida again. Once in the past he had taken his show to Florida against the will of his sponsor and had lost the sponsor because of it. Now, without a sponsor, maybe a trip down there might gain him one, one that he needed so badly. It seems to me this trip had more wishful thinking riding on it than planning. Even though he announced by way of the *Renfro Valley Bugle* and the *Sunday Morning Gatherin'* that CBS would broadcast the program from Florida for thirteen weeks, it just barely did make one Sunday. His plan was to go down without any talent but to draw from a number of past entertainers who had settled in the state of Florida. The home talent, of course, couldn't leave their jobs, so they stayed back in Renfro Valley, carrying on with the *Barn Dance* and a *Gatherin'* for the folks that showed up on Sunday morning. Even though an appeal went out across Florida to the past entertainers, some couldn't be found, and the ones that were couldn't help.

When I look back to my most disappointing year, I pretty much pinpoint 1958. And I believe it was a bad year for Mr. Lair for a different reason, even though the root cause may have been the same. In addition to the loss of CBS and WHAS, the Coon Creek Girls, an act that he had created, was no more. The little candy kitchen that had hardly made it for two years had failed and was now a souvenir shop. Just as his plan to hold the *Gatherin'* down in Florida had failed, his plan to find a Florida wintering spot for the *Barn Dance* and the *Gatherin'* was not successful. His plan to hold the *Gatherin'* in various churches around the country also had failed. In fact, his financial difficulties got to the point that he was forced to sell part of his beloved Valley, the Renfro Valley Lodge Restaurant and Tourist Court.

Even though the old Lodge had had a hard way to go and had struggled for a good many years, it was an important part of the Valley. It was thought in the beginning that the Lodge Restaurant would be the one thing that would be successful if all else failed. The thing that really mattered was that for the first time someone else would be walking through a part of his dream. He pretended that it really didn't matter. This would give him more time to do other things, put his mind to other ventures. But we knew that it did matter. He watched everything that went on across the road and strongly disapproved of any changes that were made. And there were plenty of them. There were haphazard additions here and there, and there was paint where paint didn't belong. I was real proud of the efforts the present owners made a few years ago to restore the old Lodge to its original appearance.

But John kept busy with such projects as creating a pheasant and quail hunting preserve, restocking the original Renfro Valley pond, researching his history of Rockcastle County, writing his "Tales from the Hills" article, collecting items for the pioneer museum, conducting his pony sales, and waiting for the day when radio would again take center stage and everything would be all right once more in Renfro Valley.

1960 to 1970

Years of Disappointment

T hough time continued to move, life as we knew it came to pretty much a standstill in January and February 1960, when the worst winter storm in quite a few years hit the Valley. The worry over our troubled times got a rest as the weather took over first place in our conversation. For the first time ever, I believe, the *Barn Dance* had to be canceled two weeks in a row. Many times in the dead of winter we had to move the show over to our little studio building, playing to a couple of dozen people or less. There had been cancellations from time to time over the years, but never two weeks in a row. It was about this time that John announced that Renfro Valley Folks would be returning to the air with a daily program over WCKY radio station in Cincinnati. More than likely this was just a proposal that had been made to WCKY, something maybe the two were considering rather than a done deal, as it never actually took place, but it was the kind of news that the entertainers needed right about then. Of course, we were still on the air with the *Renfro Valley Gatherin'* and were mighty thankful for the twelve stations that stood with us so faithfully. They were WJR, Detroit; WCCO, Minneapolis; WTAD, Quincy, Illinois; WIBW, Topeka, Kansas; WHAS, our mother station in Louisville, Kentucky; WAIM, Anderson, South Carolina; WLBK, De Kalb, Illinois; KBOW, Butte, Montana; WTOC, Savannah, Georgia; KTHS, Little Rock, Arkansas; and KWKH, Shreveport, Louisiana. Three of these stations are still with us today: WJR, WIBW, and WAIM.

Neither the weather, no matter how bad, nor anything else could distract us from reality for very long, especially when the last two original members of the Renfro Valley Folks said good-bye: Slim Miller

The Laurel County Boys, Renfro Valley's first bluegrass band.

in death, and Minnie Jennings (Black-eyed Susan) for a home far away out of the Valley. Not only had Susie been one of the Coon Creek Girls, she was a true sister of Lily May and Rosey and had been a faithful employee of Renfro Valley as caretaker of the music library and a big part of the *Bugle* publication since its beginning in 1943. She was a talented songwriter and vocalist, writing many of the songs still heard on our Renfro Valley *Gatherin'* today. Her talents were replaceable but, as a person, she symbolized to Mr. Lair another part of the past he couldn't hold on to. The same applied to the death of Slim Miller, the clown with the funny face and baggy britches who just happened to be able to play a fiddle to boot.

In the midst of all this came the death of Mr. Lair's only sibling, his sister, Clyde Lair Mullins, Puss, as she was so affectionately called. She was one of his biggest supporters and advisers. I'll always be thankful to Puss, as it was on her recommendation that Mr. Lair gave my buddy Clarence and me a chance on the show.

WCKY didn't come through with a daily program as was announced, but they did return us to the air with our Saturday night

Old Main Street.

Barn Dance, resulting in a renewed interest in Renfro Valley that brought us in a new act or two. One was Dave Wollum and Curly Tuttle and the Laurel County Boys. As far as I know, this was Renfro Valley's very first Bluegrass band. I read an announcement somewhere that Mr. Lair referred to Dave Wollum and Curly Tuttle and the Laurel County Boys as "so-called" Bluegrass music—so-called Bluegrass music! He never felt that Bill Monroe deserved the title of Father of Bluegrass Music. This is one time that I'll have to disagree with Mr. Lair in his thinking. He was quick to point out that the guitar, the bass, the mandolin, and the fiddle had been in place long before Bill ever thought of forming his Bluegrass Band. And, of course, this is true. But musical talent was not a part of Mr. Lair's gifts. He was a songwriter all right, but his strength was in his words, not the music. Now, he could tell if you were singing off key, and he also knew a good voice when he heard it. But because he was not a musician, I think it was easy for him to overlook the fact that Bill Monroe and his Blue-grass Boys got something new from these instruments that no one had gotten before—that style of music we now know as Bluegrass. He recognized that the Monroe brothers, Bill and Charlie, had a vocal style different than he'd ever heard before, a high lead with a tenor on top of that. After Bill and Charlie parted company, Charlie came to work here at Renfro Valley for a short time, but John Lair and Charlie Monroe just didn't hit it off for some reason or other.

There came an increase in the attendance at the *Barn Dance* during the spring of 1961; a second show was added following the WCKY broadcast. The Old Barn would only accommodate a few more than six-hundred, and tickets were still just $1 each for adults. Also, in the spring of 1961, a couple of good personal appearances came our way, making it seem like old times again. The show played Buck Lake Ranch near Angola, Indiana, and Mockingbird Hill Park near Anderson, Indiana. Bookings like these were almost a daily part of Renfro Valley's life in its first ten years. Mr. Lair cited all this as a sign that we were on our way back, as he had predicted that we would be five years earlier. But before the season was up we would know that it was not so, that things really hadn't changed in Renfro Valley.

The spring of 1962 began with the opening of the handicraft center in the Old Country Store building and the dedication of the Old Main Street that was parallel to Rt. 25 and would house the Old Country Store right next door to the Loom House, the Drug Store, and a number of other craft shops. The occasion was attended by Mr. Lair, Governor Bert Combs, and Paul Hadley, state director of arts and crafts. The old street was a great addition to the Valley but, in spite of all the fanfare, its opening was its brightest hours. Though two or three of the craft shops along the old street hung on for a few years, the craft center in the old store building was soon closed for good.

Our *Bugle* newspaper went from eight pages to sixteen, as promised, with news items about "Lula Belle and Scotty visiting Renfro Valley"; "The Renfro Valley folks dusting off, oilin' up and getting ready for a new season"; "Lily May and Rosey of the Coon Creek Girls visiting friends in Renfro Valley"; "Shorty Moore, maintenance man at Renfro Valley, boiling a buffalo head that someone had sent Mr. Lair by mail"; and "Pete Stamper moving from Lexington [where I had worked with the Prudential Insurance Company for three years] to Berea" (where I took a job with the Commonwealth Insurance Company and began to moonlight as Saturday afternoon disc jockey at WRVK).

Now, I got all this information from the March issue of the *Bugle*. It also reported that I was trying to learn the Twist. Along with Al Ballinger and Lee Earl Hysinger, I visited Nashville. I was to learn

Al Ballinger, longtime vocalist and emcee of the *Barn Dance.*

later that that trip to Nashville cost me some admiration from my friend Al Ballinger.

Al was a vocalist on the *Renfro Valley Barn Dance* and hadn't been there too long. As I lived away from Renfro Valley, I only saw Al when I came into the Valley to perform on the weekends. He knew me as a once-member of the *Red Foley Show*, Red being an idol of his and from his own town, and he knew I had recently been performing on the Grand Ole Opry. As this was Al's first trip to Nashville, he had in mind that it was going to be a trip that he would never forget. Well, I guess it turned out that way, but not as he had thought. Not only did we book one room for the three of us in the cheapest hotel we could find, we stopped at grocery stores on the way down and back for baloney, cheese, and crackers, a delicacy Lee Earl and I really enjoyed. Al was to become one of my best and closest friends, but he never viewed me as a celebrity after that.

In midsummer 1962, Mr. Lair announced that he had been invited to bring his show to perform at the Kentucky State Fair that fall. The Renfro Valley Folks would occupy a big tent set up on the fairgrounds and would hold forth with a number of daily shows along with the Saturday night *Barn Dance* and the *Sunday Morning Gatherin'*, all from the big tent.

Now, I'm sure Mr. Lair viewed this as an important showcase for the *Barn Dance*, as it had been out of the limelight for such a long time. Although we had good talent and an entertaining show for the *Barn Dance* stage in the Old Barn, this was not a show that did well on the road, and I'm sure Mr. Lair knew it. Some of the *Barn Dance* entertainers couldn't take off from their regular jobs for an entire week, and others couldn't get away at all. As it turned out, I fell into this category. My insurance job kept me close to the Valley during weekdays and, in this case, in order for Old Joe Clark to make the State Fair, I was asked to take over the WRVK programs for that weekend. What do you do when there is nothing to do with? Well, once again Mr. Lair looked to the past for the answer.

By going back and recognizing the beginning of the Renfro Valley Folks, Inc., in 1937, he could make this a twenty-fifth anniversary and would hold the first Renfro Valley homecoming. The thought was that there were enough old-timers from the *Barn Dance* stage who would show up to bring attention to the show and fill in the holes in the entertainment. No one in particular was booked, but everyone was invited, everyone they could reach. A special invitation went out to Red Foley, who was having his own troubles at the time.

On the first Saturday night of the engagement, WHAS radio station presented several of the old acts that had been heard on the Renfro Valley broadcast twenty-five years earlier. These included the Coon Creek Girls; Millie and Dolly, the Girls of the Golden West; Gene Cobb; Sleepy Marlin; and Wade Baker. Whitey Ford didn't make it for the Barn Dance but reported there on Sunday. Other old-timers appearing during the week were Little Eller, Troy Gibbs, Shorty Sheehan, Ernie Lee, Plaz Mobley, the Callaway Sisters, Coy Priddy, and Buddy and Maryanne Durham.

The death of Slim Miller on August 27, 1962, came just one month before that performance at the state fair in Louisville and, although his death was expected, I'm sure this brought a cloud of gloom for Mr. Lair during this time. Slim was the last of the original Renfro Valley Folks to perform on the Renfro Valley stage. In an editorial to the memory of Slim Miller, Mr. Lair wrote that he had had a long and

Slim Miller, top banana of the *Barn Dance*.

checkered career. He was born at Lizton, Indiana, and was adopted and raised by a neighbor to whom he gave his undying affection and respect. His foster father was an old-time fiddler, and Slim learned early to play the fiddle, developing through the years an artistry beyond that of most country fiddlers. He worked for a while with an orchestra in Indianapolis and with stock company road shows in that section of the country. Later he worked with a string band out of Knoxville, Tennessee.

One of the members of that band was Hugh Cross, who later came to work for Mr. Lair in Chicago at WLS, and it was on Hugh's recommendation that John Lair hired Slim Miller as a fiddler for the Cumberland Ridge Runners act in Chicago. Mr. Lair said Slim's natural flair for comedy had not then been developed, although it in time came to be his biggest asset and he had few equals as a sure laugh-getter. He was born Homer Edgar Miller in 1898 and was at the time of his death known from coast to coast only as Slim Miller.

A few years ago, on my way over to Owsley County in the eastern hills of Kentucky to visit my mother who lived there in a nursing home, I stopped by to see the grave site of Slim Miller, and I found it to be just exactly as John Lair described it in his editorial about Slim in the September issue of our *Renfro Valley Bugle*. He wrote, "He sleeps the last, long sleep beneath the shade of a few tall trees near the top of a hill overlooking Travelers Rest in a remote and beautiful spot hidden away in the Kentucky hills he had learned to love. A lonesome spot, perhaps, for a man who loved crowds and who could gather them about him in life, but a quiet and peaceful place to rest free from pain and await the summons for his final audition for a place in that greatest of all bands of music makers."

After the somewhat successful appearance at the Kentucky State Fair for the Renfro Valley Folks, life returned to normal. The only lasting effect was the twenty-fifth anniversary picture album that's listed among some of our treasures today. It's the silver keepsake album with 176 pictures of Renfro Valley performers of the past. Just in case you have one, you paid $1 for that copy, which, by the way, is the same price you pay today for one of our show programs filled with pictures.

The usual drop in winter attendance at our *Renfro Valley Barn Dance*, along with the worst spell of cold weather in Renfro Valley history in January 1963, caused Mr. Lair to inform us that he could no longer pay the usual $25 per person per show, and he made us a deal to split the proceeds in order to keep the show operating. The talent would take 50 percent of the gate and divide it; he would take his 50 percent and pay the expenses for heating the barn, the electricity, and so forth. All the talent except Bee Lucas went along; since we had to have Bee's services, the talent agreed to guarantee him his $25. As I recall, this worked out pretty well. We went in the hole maybe a couple or three Saturday nights; we made five or ten dollars most of the time, but we always had just as much fun as we ever had.

In the spring when we started to make up our winter's loss, John found reason to go back to the $25 guarantee, even though there were more troubled times ahead. Never again were we required or asked to share the expense of the *Barn Dance.*

Despite the fact that the *Renfro Valley Barn Dance* attendance was up and then down, up and then down, the one event that seemed to hold its own from its early success was the *Renfro Valley All-Night Gospel Sing* held the first Saturday night in August each year. This was the one event that not only brought folks from other areas outside our state but it was of interest to our local folks here in the county. A lot of the credit for its success I think should go to Jim and Wes Waggoner, who were from down Knoxville way and were founders of the Tennesseean's Quartet. Not only were they a part of the *All-Night Gospel Sing* for almost forty years, but a good part of that time they took over the booking and management until 1989. Even with seating capacity four times that of earlier years, the "Sold Out" sign still goes up in late July for our *All-Night Gospel Sing.*

Renfro Valley returned to the Kentucky State Fair again in 1963, trying to recapture some of the success it had had the year before, but it just wasn't to be. According to Old Joe Clark, the show that was made up of himself, Russ and Joe Fisher, the Farmer Sisters, Lily May, Boyd Ingram, Plaz Mobley, Deanna Sowder, and others, who played mostly to empty seats except for the Saturday night performances.

The first album of the Renfro Valley Folks featuring *Gatherin'* talent and a variety of songs heard on the *Gatherin'* was issued to mark this event. Back in the Valley, the Old Barn doors were opening up on a Friday night affair, something they called a "hootenanny." This was conducted by a group of local residents from Mt. Vernon and throughout the county and for a small fee, according to the advertisement, you could buy a seat and hear some nonprofessionals picking, singing, and putting on a show.

Now, this wasn't the first time the Old Barn had been rented to outside activity. It was used as a skating rink during the week in the

Red Brigham. In back: Don Harper, Russ Fisher; John Lair seated at desk.

forties, a successful venture for a while, so I hear. It was made available for local residents for various civic meetings, amateur shows and beauty contests. During one period that I remember, wrestling matches were held in the Old Barn. Wrestlers were handled all right, but no one could handle the audience. They became unruly and began to tear up seats and equipment so that it had to be canceled. A WRVK-sponsored Tobacco Festival in the sixties was its longest running and most successful activity.

Almost from its first opening the Old Barn was the site of at least one and sometimes two or more summer and fall revival services. These were two- and three-week services held nightly except to break for the *Renfro Valley Barn Dance* on Saturday nights. The most successful and longest running of these revivals was held by Brother Johnny Carter, a young Holiness preacher from Hamilton, Ohio.

Brother Carter was known for counties around. His group of musicians and singers numbering a dozen or more sometimes would take over our little radio station. This ensured a standing-room-only crowd throughout the revival, year after year. The preaching was hard, the singing was loud, and the Hallelujahs were many.

A lot of entertainers came and went over the years at the *Renfro Valley Barn Dance*. Some would stay a month, two months or most of one season, leaving to never return other than for a visit now and then. But a new addition to the Renfro Valley Folks in the summer of 1964 was a young man who would plant his feet solid in the Valley for a while. He was a thirty-two-year-old New Yorker by the name of William Burguiere, a Frenchman by nationality who loved good country music. He was known by his stage name of Red Brigham. Red specialized in the old-time traditional songs and knew more songs by heart than all the other *Barn Dance* talent combined. This made him a prime candidate for the Renfro Valley shows, especially the *Sunday Morning Gatherin'*. Mr. Lair considered Red a real find and thought he was one of the best singers to ever come his way. Red was a songwriter and a talented musician with an easygoing personality to boot. In spite of this, Red Brigham would be the only person I ever knew that John Lair one day not only fired but ordered out of the Valley "by sundown." Details of their troubles will come later.

Stars of the Silver Screen

Some of the best things that happen to you somehow find a way of happening when times are at their worst. I don't think I can emphasize enough just how bad it was looking for Renfro Valley folks in the early sixties. Then, from out of nowhere it seemed, a couple of gentlemen, strangers to most of us, showed up in the Valley one day to make a movie. Since they were from the city of Louisville, Kentucky, Renfro Valley was no stranger to them. I'm sure they had been watching the success of movies with a country music theme and figured Renfro Valley was ready for the starring role. I don't know if Arthur W. Standish and James F. Sullivan ever knew just how welcome they were. Along with their director friend, William Johnson from Chicago, the three musketeers took Renfro Valley without firing a shot.

The making of the movie caused more excitement in Renfro Valley in the summer of 1965 than there had been in a long, long time. The lights were bright and the cameras were in action all over the Valley; most of the action, however, was taking place on stage at the Old Barn, where the Renfro Valley performers were doing their thing. I was still trying to be an insurance salesman at that time, living and working away during the week, coming in for the *Barn Dance* and the Saturday afternoon and Sunday shifts on WRVK on the weekend. As a member of the *Barn Dance* in good standing, I had a feature spot in the movie along with some group activity here and there that required me to be on hand a few days when I was supposed to be out taking care of my insurance business. Ordinarily, this would have been all right with the company. But it just so happened that I had not been doing too well at all at selling their product.

It was about this time my boss at the insurance agency drove over to Rockcastle County to give me a badly needed helping hand. What he found didn't please him at all. He found me at Renfro Valley making a movie! The fact of the matter is, I had to do some tall talking to prevent myself from being fired right there on the spot. Well, I realized my days in the insurance business were numbered, and when I went into their office that coming Friday, I turned in my resignation. While the insurance business is an honorable business, as my friends Steve Gulley and Mark Laws can tell you, they will also tell you that some of us are just not cut out for it.

Speaking of selling insurance, I'll never forget the first week on the job by myself. I was trained by a staff manager, or assistant manager, and I tried to pick up from him all the little do's and don'ts along the way. My greeting, I realized, was a little bit outdated. I was in the habit of saying "Hidy Do." So, if I was going to be a distinguished insurance salesman, I should update my greeting. I decided I would say "Good Morning" or "Good Afternoon," whichever applied. My first try didn't turn out too well. I walked up on the porch, knocked on the door and had every intention of saying "Good Morning." The lady came to the door and, just as I started to speak, she said, "Hello." And I said, "Goolo." I didn't sell anything there. Between there and my next stop, which was a few doors down the street, I practiced up on my "Good Morning, Good Morning, Good Morning." I walked up on the porch, opened the storm door and knocked on the door, then stepped back, going over in my mind just what I was going to say. I thought I heard the door open, so I turned and gave my best "Good Morning." I was so pleased with myself, but there was no one there. What I had heard was the storm door closing. Then the door opened and the lady said, "Good Morning." I said, "Hidy Do." I didn't sell anything there either. A few more doors on down the street, I walked up on this rather small porch. I knocked on the door, stepped back to go over in my mind again whether it was going to be Good Morning, Hello, Hidy Do, or what. I stepped back too far and fell off into the shrubbery! No one came to the door, which was my only good break of the day. I stayed in the insurance business for six long years, but it was downhill from there on out.

But back to Renfro Valley. When Mr. Lair learned that I had resigned from my job, he offered me full-time employment again at WRVK. This would be the second time I had gone to work for WRVK, so I was hoping I would do better than the first time, which only lasted six months. Never in my wildest dreams did I think that this time around it would be for twenty-one years and six months. Finally, I had found something I really enjoyed doing. The work of a disc jockey is a whole lot like performing on stage; I guess for a change I was a full-time entertainer once again. It was my experience with the recording equipment at the radio station that made it possible for me to go to work in the production of the Renfro Valley *Gatherin'* in 1966, a job that I still hold today.

When that big movie was completed, we finished out the year in high spirits, I'll have to say. The Valley had only the feel of good times. We had no way of knowing just what kind of a job our picture makers had done, but a chance to be in any kind of a movie seldom comes along in a lifetime. At least things in Renfro Valley were feeling good again. Someone mentioned somewhere along the line that this might have been just a flimflam, wondering if there was even any film in the camera. Personally, a time or two I was kind of hoping there was not. As I was doing stand-up comedy, it was decided my part would definitely be filmed in front of the live Saturday night *Barn Dance*. Well, I was all for this. It made sense, but I soon found out that it was not your typical *Barn Dance* audience. First, the local folks in and around Renfro Valley were as interested in being in the movie as we were. They had bought most of all the seats, which meant that I either knew or was known by about 75 percent of the audience, and that's not good when you're trying to be funny. Second, wireless microphones had not yet been invented and the microphone that I was wearing on my shirtfront ran down inside my shirt, down my pants, and out my left britches leg, and from there to who knows where. I felt like my walk-out to center stage might have been the funniest part of my routine. When we were about halfway into my routine, the cameraman yelled, "Cut." He was out of film. He instructed me to pick up where I had quit. But, there wasn't a starting place where I quit. I went back a little further than he intended for me to, and I understand this caused quite a bit of confusion when he got back to Chicago to do his editing. I understand I almost ended up on the cutting-room floor.

The movie turned out to be pretty much as it was intended to be, I think. There was really no story line or plot, just a few scenery shots of the Valley, a few minutes with Mr. Lair in his office in the museum and broadcast building, which set the stage for what was to come. The rest of the movie was sort of a scripted version of the *Renfro Valley Barn Dance* with a fiddle competition featured throughout. Lily

Movie Promo.

May of the Coon Creek Girls, Sleepy Marlin, and Buddy Durham, all fiddlers from the past, came back to join Bee Lucas and Ralph Marcum. If there was a highlight to the movie, I suppose this would have been it.

A few other former Renfro Valley Folks returned to take a part in our movie. Jeanne Gibson was already back working with us, and Plaz Mobley, who was a mountain lawyer over in the eastern part of the state, paid us a visit, treating us to his brand of mountain ballad. We really couldn't afford to let Plaz on the show other than maybe a couple times a year. His favorite song was "Barbara Allen," and he always insisted on doing at least twenty-six verses.

Estill McNew and his Kentucky Briarhoppers brought the movie to life with their square dancing. Miss Ginger Callahan was another entertainer from the early Renfro Valley days who made it back for the movie. And there was Roy Starkey, who was really a western singer. He'd worked with Mr. Lair before, and I think spent a little bit of time in front of the movie cameras out in Hollywood doing some of the "singing westerns." Soon after our movie was completed and long before it was ever released, Roy had a heart attack during one of our *Barn Dances* and was rushed to the hospital in nearby Mount Vernon. I remember getting a call the next day from Doc Jack Lewis and remember Doc's words. He said, "I'm sorry to have to tell you we lost your buddy last night." Sometime during the night, after seemingly doing real well, Roy had had another heart attack and died.

With one exception, none of the rest of us had ever been to Hollywood, but we enjoyed acting like Hollywood stars there for a while. That one exception was Lee Earl Hysinger. He didn't sing, dance, or play music. He had never been on the *Barn Dance* or *Jamboree*, but he loved the spotlight more than anyone I ever knew. He was a good friend of many of the entertainers; he was the first one to lend me a hand after my arrival in the Valley. It was the third or fourth appearance on the *Barn Dance* for my buddy Clarence and me. We had worked out a rambunctious skit that called for me to take a tumble down the stage steps. I was young and wiry; I did a good fall. I landed just a few feet from the front row seats at the left of the stage. Although I didn't need the assistance, a member of the audience in the front row helped me up and helped me back up the steps onto the stage. I was soon to learn that that was my first meeting with Lee Hysinger. We became friends and started hanging out together.

It wasn't long until Mr. Lair sent word that he needed to see me in his office. When I got there he informed me that I had picked a bad character as a friend and that if I wanted to be successful in Renfro Valley, I should make some changes in the company I was keeping. He went on to say that the Hysinger boy was no good—a troublemaker, a drunk, and a number of other things. Now, the Hysinger family lived up at the head of Renfro Creek, an old and respectable family of hard-working folks, but Lee Earl, according to Mr. Lair, was the bad apple of the bunch. Lee Earl's uncle, Jack Hysinger, was the guard or doorman at the stage door of the *Barn Dance* and would let just about anyone in backstage except his nephew, Lee Earl.

What Mr. Lair and most others didn't know or probably would not have believed, considering how mean Lee Earl had been, was that there had been a change in his life. I only heard about Lee Earl the

Lee Earl Hysinger and Friends: Speedy (Joe) Clark, Huntz Hall, Lee Earl, and Leo Gorcey (The Bowery Boys).

outlaw. He was already walking the straight and narrow when we met, but his bad reputation continued to follow him. Lee Earl was drawing partial disability from the armed services, allowing him to pick and choose his employment—or unemployment, which was his choice most of the time. He had a talent for picking up bargains in good used clothing and jewelry. At one time most of us entertainers on the *Barn Dance* were wearing a ring or watch or maybe both supplied by Lee Earl Hysinger. And we dressed a little bit better having Lee Earl as a friend. One of the finest suits I ever owned in my life was purchased from Lee Earl for $20. He didn't try to make a profit; he just enjoyed doing the favors.

He didn't like to loan you anything, but he would give you the shirt off his back, and the fact of the matter is, he did once upon a time. I mentioned a couple of times that I liked the shirt he was wearing, and he said he'd like for me to have it as a gift. It was the most comfortable shirt I had ever owned, and I wore it to so many places. I once could have told you just where those places were. After I had it about six months, I had reason to think back and make a note of the many places I had been seen in that shirt. That was after someone with a good eye for detail informed me that the shirt Lee Earl and I had been wearing was really a maternity blouse. I never did find out if this was a little prank that he pulled on me or if he, too, really didn't know the difference. Either way, it didn't matter; it brought us so much amusement in the forty years we were friends. Making friends was his most outstanding talent, and he used that talent to the fullest. His friends and acquaintances were found in high places—in politics, show business—and with ordinary folks and the downtrodden. That talent, along with his desire to be in show business of some kind, took him to Hollywood in the 1950s, where he managed to get a card from the Actors Guild and a walk-on part in the movie *The Caddy* with Jerry Lewis and Dean Martin. He landed a similar part in *Country Music on Broadway*, which starred most of the biggest names in Nashville at the time. He helped to get Old Joe Clark a featured part in that same movie. And in our movie, it's Lee Earl playing the part of one of the revenuers in a raid on the moonshine still. In *Country Music on Broadway* he played the role of a theater doorman in New York. For the part of one summer, John Lair hired Lee Earl as the real doorman at the stage entrance of the Old Barn here in Renfro Valley. He was proud of the job, even if it wasn't in front of the footlights. After all, it was Renfro Valley, and it was show business. But I doubt if Lee Earl ever understood the significance of those two months, for those months proved that he had left that outlaw reputation far behind.

Lee Earl died of emphysema in March 1990. He couldn't sing, dance, or play music; he could just make friends. I can't help but wonder if those of us who do sing, dance, and play do it better for having once had a friend like Lee Earl Hysinger.

We had a private showing of the movie over in nearby Berea, and then there was the big premier in the city of Louisville. On the day of the premier we all loaded up and headed for Louisville. It was our understanding that Clarence Walls would be driving up later. Clarence was a young man from over around Danville who had been doing a number on our *Barn Dance* for just a short time before the movie was being made. He wasn't that swift of a vocalist, but his portrayal of Old Joe Clark's oldest, knuckle-headed boy was flawless. If anyone ever enjoyed his fifteen minutes of fame any more than Clarence Walls, I don't know who it was.

Now it wasn't Clarence's first time in town, but it was his first time in the big city of Louisville, and he stayed longer than he really intended to. He took with him the address of the theater and was told the general area of the town where it was located. Clarence set out to find it on his own. He had been told that parking spaces at the theater might be a little scarce, so he decided to park his car and leave the driving to someone else. He pulled into a service station, locked his car, and called a cab. The cab took him to the theater with no problem, then departed. It wasn't until Clarence was ready to leave and was asked by whomever was going to drop him off at his car that he realized he had not made a note of the street or even the name of the service station. Well, I understand that after about a tank of gas and a stop at McDonald's for supper, they finally spotted Clarence's chariot still parked where he'd left it ten hours earlier.

I still watch the movie on my VCR once in a while, and I always see things that remind me of those little things that took place behind the scenes that bring back fond memories. The cap that Clarence Walls wore was my cap; I loaned it to him just for his part in the show. He didn't return it. Marie Farmer returned it, twenty years later. I asked her how she'd come by it; she just giggled and said, "That's for me to know and you to find out." I never did find out.

And if you had looked closely at the suit I was wearing, the lapel pin was really a license plate bolt placed there by Rube Anglin of Anglin's Auto Sales, Hamilton, Ohio, who sold me enough cars that I was able to write my car song, "Cheva-Kaiser-Olds-Mo-Laca-Stude-War-Linco-Baker."

The Boss Steps Down

With the excitement of our new-found fame, something else was taking place. I can't for the life of me remember the first time that I heard that John just might sell Renfro Valley, but we began to hear talk of his retirement; after all, he was seventy-one. I remember hearing that Mrs. Lair would like to settle down, maybe in Florida, but I don't think any of us took any of this talk too seriously. Maybe because we just couldn't imagine Renfro Valley without John Lair at the helm. Even after I learned that there was a country music concern down in Tennessee interested in the Valley, I still never believed that a change of ownership would come about. I feel that pressure from family and friends and the fact that attendance to the *Renfro Valley Barn Dance* was just not improving forced Mr. Lair to offer Entertainment Corporation of America (ECA) of Goodletsville, Tennessee, a two-year lease of the Valley for 1966-68 with an option of purchase. One provision that he stipulated was that during these two years, ECA, which owned a booking office and had access to quite a bit of country music talent, would bring a star entertainer or a guest entertainer to the *Barn Dance* each Saturday night. This had never been a part of John Lair's thinking before, and the only reason I can see that he would have had any interest in this taking place was that this star treatment might bring the Valley enough badly needed publicity that it would be to his benefit when he took back his operations in two years.

I do not believe John Lair ever thought the Valley would really change hands. He had agreed to stay on as emcee of the *Barn Dance* and writer and narrator of the *Gatherin'*. I don't know if he was retained as general manager or not, but I do know he considered himself sort of in that role. ECA had sent one of its own people to act as overseer and, if not then, later, general manager. This person was none other than musician and vocalist Wade "Pug Nose" Ray. This put the Renfro Valley talent in an uncomfortable position. We wanted to cooperate with the new folks in hopes that their presence in the Valley might be the answer Renfro Valley needed. And, at the same time, we felt we owed allegiance to John Lair, the man who made our jobs possible in the first place and who was still in a management role. Everything seemed to be working out okay as the most drastic change in the history of the *Renfro Valley Barn Dance* took place. Never before had Renfro Valley featured an outside guest every Saturday night, although it did make a guest spot available for young unknown talent who were coming up.

The word was out that Nashville was buying Renfro Valley. The ECA folks involved had nothing to do with the Grand Ole Opry anymore but were prominent in country music. They were Ray Price, Willie Nelson, Hank Cochran, and Hal Smith, who was the president. Some of the guests who appeared during those two years were Jeanne Sealy, Jack Green, Hank Cochran, Grandpa and Ramona Jones, entertainer-songwriter Dave Kirby, Ray Price and the Cherokee Cowboys, Tex Ritter, and Ernest Tubb and the Texas Troubadours, just to name a few. A couple of comedians came north on a few occasions, James "Goober" Buchanan and a fellow by the name of Bun Wilson.

The lesser-known solo acts usually had a spot within our *Barn Dance* show if they didn't demand too much, otherwise the Renfro Valley folks did their hour, hour and fifteen minutes, and then we would clear the stage, turning the remaining portion of the show over to our guests. This brought drums to the stage of the *Barn Dance* for the very first time. Of course, Ray Price and the Cherokee Cowboys used drums. I do have a picture of Lois Johnson on stage and there is a drummer sitting behind her. Lois Johnson, in addition to her solo work, was best known for her duets with Hank Williams Jr. and her featured spot on the Ernest Tubb television show.

Hal Smith made sure that we had a guest on stage every Saturday night. Hal was known for his crossing every T and dotting every I, and somewhere along the line I suppose Mr. Lair saw that he had every intention of exercising his option to purchase the Valley. It wasn't too long 'til John was voicing his displeasure with most everything that went on. Most of the Renfro Valley talent, although they sympathized with his feelings, were for the change of ownership but kept their feelings to themselves. The crowds had begun to pick up, and there were a few little things going on that made it look as if Renfro Valley might have some kind of a future after all. But one old boy who didn't learn this lesson was Red Brigham. Red made the mistake of taking sides with ECA too early when John Lair was voicing displeasure of ECA's decisions. Red overestimated the value ECA had for him at that time and underestimated the power that John Lair still wielded in Renfro Valley. To say it got hot between the two is an understatement. The fact of the matter is, John Lair flat out fired Red Brigham on the spot and ordered him off the property immediately. This wasn't the way it was supposed to turn out, and Red flatly refused to go. But, finally, someone made Red realize that there was serious trouble ahead if he didn't go. John told me later that he was prepared for the situation to get worse and for only the second time he had put a pistol in his desk drawer just in case it was needed. The other time, he told me, was because of some trouble he was having with Charlie Monroe. Ann Henderson told me recently that her father was just being conservative, that the pistol was there on quite a few occasions. We all felt sorry for Red. He had banked so much on this being the big break for his floundering career. They say time heals all wounds, and I guess it does. This was a pretty deep one, yet about ten years later Mr. Lair made an effort to get Red Brigham back to the Valley. It didn't work out, but it did show that forgiveness had taken place on both sides.

ECA exercised its option to purchase Renfro Valley in 1968. I suppose when you are all of something for so long, it's mighty hard to be just a part, especially when decisions are being made that you don't agree with. John resigned from all activity in the Valley, but before he left, he hired Glen Pennington to come back to emcee the *Renfro Valley Barn Dance.* I never understood why he felt he needed Glen back. It was not just for his emcee talents, I know, anymore than that was Glen's reason for coming back. I heard, though I can't say for sure it's true, that Glen agreed to emcee the show for all of $10 a week. If true, it shows that it was John who wanted him there and not Hal Smith. I'm pretty sure Hal would have offered a little more than this if it had been his idea. Glen was looking for a foot in the Renfro Valley door, and this gave him all the toe-hold he needed to be in and out of the ownership of the Valley for the next twenty-five years. Mr. Lair's departure from the Valley was felt most of all on the *Sunday Morning Gatherin'* program, which was then in its twenty-fifth year and had had no writer, director, or narrator other than John Lair.

We were left with a problem, but one that was easily solved, as we had in the music library all the *Gatherin'* recordings since 1960. We simply took out of the programs anything that would indicate it was from an earlier broadcast, and Marie Farmer and I read into the show current birthday and anniversary announcements. This got us through the winter months as far as the radio broadcasts were concerned.

I was asked to take over Mr. Lair's place on stage at the live performances. These reruns were used for just a few weeks until Entertainment Corporation of America contracted with Grand Ole Opry announcer Grant Turner to write and narrate the radio portion of the *Gatherin'*. This arrangement with Grant doing the radio broadcasts and my doing the live *Gatherin'*, continued for approximately two years.

The Gatherin'

The simplicity of the *Gatherin's* format didn't come about out of necessity; it was written in and became its strongest feature, though the least understood. Mr. Lair's approach was to convey to the listening audience life in this little settlement as uncomplicated and never-changing in style. It was truly the "valley where time stands still." I have a picture of the cast taken sometime around the first broadcast. It was nine years on up the road before I watched my first program. My first impression was not of the program itself, but of how different the atmosphere around the *Gatherin'* was from the *Barn Dance* performance just the night before. Where just a few hours earlier on the very same stage these same entertainers were carefree, laughing, squealing, making joyful noises, having a good time, now they talked in a whisper, tip-toed around the stage, smiled nervously as they played and sang so pretty.

But, this was not just live radio, this was now live on the CBS network! This was 1952 and General Foods was paying the bill. They were paying two New Yorkers, Johnny and Barbara DeMott, to produce the program, and they were the most nervous of all. Only John Lair seemed to be cool, calm, and collected. But why be nervous? What if someone forgot the words to their song and the birds in the barn loft were chirping louder than the singers? What if the bellows on the old parlor organ were squeaking and the old clock on the wall said you had more time than you thought you would have? Why, we'll just read a few more birthdays and anniversary announcements. After all, it's not like you were doing a radio program. It's just a gatherin' of local folks singing and talking about local things just picked up by

Cast picture at the first *Gatherin'* broadcast from the little Redbud School-house September 5, 1943, over the CBS Southern Network. From left: Glen Pennington, Tommy Covington, Rhuel Thomas, unknown, Flossie Thomas, Virginia Sutton, Judy and Jean Dickerson, Wade Baker (with guitar), Patty Flye. Standing in door: Al Staas and John Lair. On the right, seated: Norma Coffee, unknown, Susie Ledford. In back, standing: Lily May Ledford, Elsie Behrens, Miss Ruth Mullins, Bob Thompson, Jerry Behrens, Troy Gibbs, and Bob Simmons.

radio. This was the format and personality John Lair was creating for the *Gatherin'*. He made sure the first broadcast was held in the little Redbud Schoolhouse, symbolic of the meetings that the early settlers had held there in days gone by.

The *Sunday Morning Gatherin'* for Ballard & Ballard first aired on September 8, 1943. From the beginning the *Gatherin'* was transmitted by telephone wire that was locally owned here in Rockcastle County by the Dees Telephone Company that operated within the county. It was then picked up by another telephone company that took it on to WHAS radio station in Louisville and later on around the country by way of the CBS network. It was the practice to clear this line a few minutes before air time to make sure there were no problems.

The *Gatherin'* cast through most of the fifties. Seated, from left: Roy Davidson; Susan, Lily May, and Rosey (the Coon Creek Girls); Flossie Thomas; and Jerry Behrens. Standing, from left: Slim Miller; Ray Sosby; Claud Sweet; Rhuel Thomas; John Lair; Miss Ruth Mullins; Robert Thompson; Glen Pennington; and Dick Dickenson.

One morning on my first visit to the *Gatherin'*, Johnny DeMott needed to talk to his agency in New York about the commercial they were going to do. When he tried to get the exchange in Mt. Vernon just up the road about three miles, he couldn't get an answer. Panic set in. The question was, would we be able to get on the air in just a few minutes. I was only visiting the *Gatherin'* that morning, and when Mr. Lair spotted me backstage, he pitched me his car keys and told me to hurry up to Mt. Vernon and let them know we were calling. When I got there I found that they had already answered the ring. The lady apologized and told me that they were eating breakfast and were not expecting a call that early. The exchange was operated out of a private residence at the time. Of course, WHAS kept a stand-by program on hand just in case we were not able to get on the air for one reason or the other.

I left the Valley in 1954, and when I returned four years later the *Gatherin'* had been dropped from the CBS network but had gained such a loyal audience that a number of stations wanted to continue it. This required taping the program in advance and mailing it out to

Gatherin' mid-sixties: Bee Lucas, Adaline and Don Harper, Marie and Bess Farmer, John Lair, Ann Honeycutt, Hazel Farmer, Jo Fisher, Bob Thompson, Virginia Sutton, Red Brigham.

various stations. All these arrangements were made and put into play before it was taken off the network. The fact is that the program has been broadcast over some stations, somewhere in the country, every week for the past fifty-five years, making it the third oldest continuous radio broadcast in the nation.

If you were a member of the *Gatherin'* cast, you were treated to a special meeting with Mr. Lair each Sunday morning following the program. The past, present, and future, the good news and the bad news concerning the Valley were always discussed. The news couldn't have been worse than when they learned that the sponsor was moving their money from radio to the TV networks. CBS would continue to carry the *Gatherin'* for some time on a sustaining basis, but no other sponsor stepped up to take over. Fortunately, the *Gatherin'* had built such a loyal audience in a dozen areas of the country that these stations made contact with Renfro Valley about the possibility of carrying the *Gatherin'* on a delayed basis. I have said before and I will say again, I believe if WJR in Detroit had dropped the *Gatherin'* at that time, there's a good chance there would not be a Renfro Valley as we know it today. This was a 50,000-watt clear channel station covering much of Michigan, Wisconsin, Illinois, Ohio, Indiana, and southern Canada, where a good many of our visitors lived and worked and to this day provide a loyal base of listeners and visitors to Renfro Valley.

Jim Gaskin and Grant Turner, the only two permanent
hosts of the *Gatherin'* except John Lair.

These folks knew that the Valley was still alive if not as well as we
could have been.

My first direct involvement with the *Gatherin'* came in about 1966,
when the recording engineer failed to show up one Saturday afternoon. Mr. Lair asked me if I thought I could handle the job; I told him
no. He said, "Good, that means you'll try harder." We got through it
somehow, and from then on I was on call whenever I was needed. It
was at the change of ownership in the Valley when I was given the job
permanently.

Gatherin' mid-eighties: from left, Curt Caldwell, Eunice and Bee Lucas, Vester Parker, Susan Tomes, Grady Hockett, Edith Priddy, Patty Towery, Coy Priddy, Patty Flye, and Virginia Sutton.

Now I'm aware that many of you who are reading this have never heard the *Gatherin'*, and you may be wondering why all the fuss? Well, first, it's unique in many ways. It's not a country music program, even though it is performed by country music talent. It's not a pop show, in spite of the fact that 75 percent of the songs that find their way onto the show are old pop classics, and it's not a gospel or church program, yet many of our listeners refer to it as "the Sunday Morning Service."

It seems the *Gatherin'* has an appeal to a wide range of people but with one thing in common. John Lair expressed it best in that first program, and I quote, "Folks, we talked about this program a right smart Friday morning on the air and I hope we made it plain just what we wanted to do in these little *Sunday Morning Gatherin's*. Well, it's very simple. We want to put on the air the bits of sentiment and precious memories that have made your life a little better, the load a little easier to carry. We all like to remember and we all like to look back down the road we've traveled and recall the things we've

The Renfro Valley *Gatherin'* 1992: Vester Parker, Virginia Sutton, Jim Gaskin, Susan Tomes, Jeff Parker, Dale Ann Bradley, Clyde Foley, Steve Gulley.

heard and seen, the people we've known and loved, memories, some sweet, some sad, but all precious."

For some folks it is the beginning of their Sunday morning routine. For others, it marks the end of a pleasant weekend in Renfro Valley. To one person it's a country music program; to another it's a church service. Taken in one light, it is continually changing; seen in another, it has remained the same for over half a century. In those community meetings of long ago, each person in attendance came for a different reason: one to visit with neighbors, another to sing a lively tune, one to catch up on the local news and some to enjoy a hymn or an inspirational message. Today's *Gatherin'* is still just that, many things to many people. But it is, and always will be, a special place to everyone, a place where you are always welcome, where you can hear the old songs as well as the new, and where you can find, we hope, your own unique Renfro Valley memories to take home with you.

Then there was the story of Miss Mamie Hargis of Texas. In the closing years of World War II, she wrote to Mr. Lair to tell him about listening to the *Gatherin'* with her fiancé and hearing the song "I'll Be

With You When the Roses Bloom Again." She said they made that their song. A friend had made a recording of it, and she had planned to not play it until he returned from that foreign land. She asked to hear the song on the program one more time, as the War Department had informed her that her love was missing in action and believed dead. She said she would listen and pretend that he was with her. In the mail the day before the program was to air another letter came saying she wouldn't have to pretend after all. She had been informed that he was alive and was on his way home. The Renfro Valley Folks sung the song for Miss Hargis that morning in hopes that her love had made it in time to share the song with her.

Heading up the *Sunday Morning Gatherin'* are two fine talents placed in their position at the table by John Lair himself, Susan Tomes and Jim Gaskin. At this writing, Susan has already chalked up eighteen years on the program, which is quite a compliment. Mr. Lair chose Jim to fill his shoes as narrator, and I know Mr. Lair would be proud of the fine job that he's done.

I'm proud to say Renfro Valley and our *Gatherin'* are in the best health they have ever been. We are at our peak, and through the promotional efforts of Cindy Roberts, special events director, and her staff, we're growing every month. Over the years the power of the *Gatherin'* has been strong, having set records for the amount of mail received from one commercial announcement and causing two automobile giants, Ford and Buick, to lay claim to having manufactured the "bell" used at the close of the show. Actually, it's a brake drum that makes the bell-like sound. Donations from the *Gatherin'* helped to build a home for wayward boys down in Florida in the early fifties, and before there was any outside help for poor families in this community, listeners to the *Gatherin'* also helped provide a Christmas of toys, clothing, and food for hundreds of poor Appalachian families over a period of about twenty years by mere mention of need expressed by Mr. Lair on the weekly show.

Today, folks who attend the *Gatherin'* in person on Sunday mornings find the Old Barn theater warm or cool, whichever is appropriate at the time. The lights are on, the microphones set, the old parlor organ is in its place, songbooks are ready, and the sound made just right, all seen to by one Hans Lindbloom. In the early eighties Hans was living in California and just happened to hear on the radio one Sunday morning a program that caught his attention, and he continued to listen. It turned out to be the Renfro Valley *Sunday Morning*

Coy Priddy, Hans Lindbloom, Jim Gaskin, Jerry Isaacs.

Gatherin'. He liked it so well he listened again the next week and the next week, and a picture of a simpler way of life in a real community off in the hills of Kentucky began to dance in his head: the redbuds and dogwoods in the spring, summer roses and fishin' holes, technicolor hills in the fall, and lots of banjo and fiddle music to keep you warm in the winter.

These pictures just wouldn't go away. Hans, who was just about to retire at a fairly young age, decided to see for himself. The first visit was followed by two, three, then four, and finally he made it permanent. Since coming to work for Renfro Valley Folks some years ago he has met and married his wife, Betty, who was a shopkeeper and candlemaker in our village. His position as computer programmer for the company keeps him at his desk behind closed doors most of the time, but when Sunday morning rolls around, you'll find Hans attending to his first love, the Renfro Valley *Gatherin'*.

You heard us say many times that the Renfro Valley entertainers are a family. I feel like the *Gatherin'* crew is kind of special, a family within the family. They have shared so many experiences that only this program could provide.

Who's on First?

The *Barn Dance* was faring a whole lot better at the close of the sixties than in the recent past. Nick Foley had joined the cast. Nick was from over in the Berea area, hometown of the late Red Foley; Nick claimed to be a distant cousin of Red. And the Bluegrass Drifters, Renfro Valley's second Bluegrass band, was expanding its role on the show. They would establish themselves as a permanent fixture in one way or the other for a long time to come. The group included lead singer/guitar player John Cosby; Bill Ferguson, playing bass; Charles Durham, playing fiddle; and Vester Parker on banjo. The Parker Brothers, along with Vester's son Jeff Parker, would hold down the Bluegrass spot on the show until the early nineties.

Of course, Old Joe Clark, the Farmer Sisters, Ralph Marcum, and Bee Lucas were still on the show. Don Harper had left to pursue other interests, but we didn't have to go far to fill his place. Just up the road two or three miles was a fine guitar player by the name of Glenn Thompson. Glenn had been leaning toward the rock 'n roll of that day and time. He agreed to tone it down a little bit and come on the *Renfro Valley Barn Dance* and *Sunday Morning Gatherin'*. Al Ballinger, another product of Berea, a fine country vocalist, was also holding down part of the emcee work on the *Barn Dance*. Slim Miller had been responsible for bringing Al to the show a few years earlier.

Some changes were taking place in other areas of the Valley. Ralph Marcum had taken over the duties as editor of the *Bugle*. The *Gatherin'* was up around forty stations for the first time in a dozen years. The Renfro Valley Tape Club, operated by Reuben and Retha Powell of Springfield, Ohio, had its beginning, and thanks to their total devo-

The Bluegrass Drifters in 1965: Bill Ferguson, Vester Parker, Charlie Durham, John Cosby.

tion to the music of Renfro Valley, there is preserved for future generations quite a collection of Renfro Valley history and song. We have only a few of his tapes; his entire collection was donated to Berea College at Reuben's death.

The Friday night "Hootenanny" that we mentioned earlier, promoted by local residents and held in the Old Barn, didn't meet with too much success. We gave a try to a Friday night square dance or two, and then for the first time on a regular basis, the first time that I recall ever hearing about, an outside country music show came in and took over a regular spot on Friday night. Bonnie Lou and Buster, well-known artists from the Knoxville and Pigeon Forge area of Tennessee, tried their hand at establishing a Friday night show. In spite of the fact that they had TV exposure out of Knoxville and the best of comedy by Red and Fred, a comedy team also from Knoxville, producing just an all-around good country music show, they, too, gave it up as a lost cause after a few weeks. It began to look as if Renfro Valley, with its rural location, would never be more than just a Saturday night *Barn Dance,* and I was one of the strongest believers. Fact of the matter is, I expressed my views a few times, until present owners proved us all wrong. Now our shows, Wednesday through Sunday, boast success we would never dreamed of having. Many times our Wednesday and Thursday night shows fill as many seats in the Old Barn as our Saturday night shows did prior to the expansion that took place in the nineties.

Years ago, ticket sales, information requests, museum admission, *Bugle* subscriptions, souvenir hymn books, postcard sales, maintenance, and publicity were all handled at one desk by one person who also served as Mr. Lair's private secretary. Her name was Virginia Bray. She came to work at 8:00 A.M. and left at 4:00 P.M., Monday through Friday, working a little overtime on Saturday.

However, there were lots of folks who would stop in at Renfro Valley to get information and tour the museum after 4:00 P.M. And this led to my first job outside my act on the *Barn Dance* stage. I was asked to keep the museum open a couple of hours each afternoon. The museum was laid out in three sections on the second floor of the big, log building. You reached the big double doors by a flight of stairs that ran up from the breezeway. Just inside these doors, was a small waist-high table for the roll of tickets, change box, and a cigar box for the ticket stubs. The visitors started their tour in the large room that ran almost the full length of the building. The main room housed a little bit of everything from the life of the pioneers plus a whole lot of guns. Mr. Lair had an interest in old guns and in odd, strange and curious firearms. There was a rifle that had been used in a certain Civil War battle, a sword owned by a famous general, a weapon used at the Battle of the Alamo, and even one owned by the head of a mountain clan and leader of a feud. A part of my job was to guide the visitor through the museum pointing out items of interest. On a few rare occasions I was privileged to tour with Mr. Lair and hear the details of these stories as only he knew them and could tell them.

Just off the far end of the main room was the Music Room, with a collection of odd, strange, and curious musical instruments and music boxes. There was an early juke box that was electrically operated. The records were metal disks with prongs that touched certain reels as the disks turned, playing a variety of tunes. Then there was a wind-up model that I was authorized to operate for the guests if they asked; I always managed to lead the conversation around in such a way that they would ask. Most of the folks who stopped by during the weekdays had not seen our Saturday night *Barn Dance* show, so I also led the conversation around in such a way as to let them know that I was one of the stars. From the music room you retraced your steps, finding things you missed earlier and taking another look at things that especially caught your interest. The last section just to the right of the entrance door was filled with items pertaining to all types of work. Two of the larger items were the handmade wooden hay baler and the old moonshine still.

I think the price of a ticket was maybe 25 or 35 cents. I had been told by the bookkeeper to sell a ticket, make change, tear the ticket down the middle, give half to the customer, drop the other half in the box that was there for that purpose. Each ticket had a number and at the end of the day a count of the tickets and the money I had on hand would tell what kind of business we had done and provide a check of the cash, a control to see that all the money was properly accounted for.

I'll never forget the day that Uncle Sam caught me breaking the rules just a little bit. It was a slow day; I had only five or six customers all afternoon. I was about ready to close up and turn in my count to the bookkeeper, who was downstairs working late that day, when twenty-three people appeared at the door, all in one party, to go through the museum. I never had that many all at one time before, and I took the shortest route to getting them in. I totaled up the price, received their payment, gave change, and showed them through the museum. But I had failed to tear the tickets off the roll. Suddenly, in the door came Mr. Nester, the bookkeeper, and two nicely dressed gentlemen who were introduced to me as the IRS. There had been some tax problems in the Valley, and they were there to close down the museum just as soon as the guests that were going through had left. So, to keep from causing any alarm, the two IRS agents began to tour the museum on their own and left me with Mr. Nester at the door. Mr. Nester managed to ask me in a whisper if everything was in order. I told him everything was except I had not been able to tear those twenty-three tickets off. He went pale and said to me to manage somehow to tear those tickets off without being seen. This I accomplished, but I wasn't able to tear them in two. I went downstairs out of sight where I proceeded to tear the tickets in two, knowing that I could not give the half to the customers. I brought the half that belonged in the box back upstairs and managed to slip them in. Mr. Nester asked me what I did with the other halves. When I told him that I threw them under his desk, I thought the man was going to faint. He sent me back downstairs to retrieve those tickets, and when I got back upstairs the IRS asked me for the money that I had taken in that day. Well, as it turned out, I had made change out of my own money and I ended up having to admit to the whole mix-up in order to get my money back. That was my first and only run-in with the IRS, and at such a tender young age, too.

I was always sorry that the Pioneer Museum was not able to keep its home in the Valley. A good part of its contents had been donated and was not included in the sale to Entertainment Corporation of America. These items were eventually stored on John Lair's own property, and it became necessary to dispose of them at auction at a later date. Many of our visitors still come searching for the old museum.

When the rebuilding of the Valley got under way in 1989, arrangements were made for Renfro Valley Folks to lease from a private individual a large collection of country music memorabilia that filled both stories of the big museum building, which had just been doubled in size. The collection contained personal items from people all the way from Elvis Presley to Old Joe Clark. Once more the museum became a Renfro Valley attraction. A year later the owner of the collection, who was in debt to the IRS for back taxes, defaulted. The IRS took the museum contents and sold them at an auction to settle the tax claim. A few items did not belong to the leaser but did have real close ties to Renfro Valley. We were able to recover those items before the auction and return them to their rightful place. One was the old Western Electric console that was used to broadcast the CBS and WHAS radio programs out of the Valley and was later used by WRVK radio station for its first twenty years of service. The old console is now on display at the John Lair Theater. Another was that big aluminum bass fiddle that is displayed at the side of the stage in the New Barn theater and used from time to time.

When Renfro Valley changed hands in 1968 there was one record album to Renfro Valley's credit. It was an album of the *Sunday Morning Gatherin'* put together to coincide with Renfro Valley's return to the state fair for an appearance in 1963. The new owners, Entertainment Corporation of America, put out a second album recorded in 1969, again of the *Gatherin'*. For the cover photograph we gathered on the steps of the little Redbud Schoolhouse, which had been the location of the first broadcast in 1943.

This album was followed by a single by Wade Ray and a comedy album that I'm proud of as much for the cover as for its contents. The cover was a cartoon picture of some of my earliest material by an artist in the Louisville area.

For a while it seemed the new owners of the Valley were making some progress. J. Hal Smith, president of ECA, and his partner Hank

Cochran had taken full ownership of the Valley. As they were absentee owners with main offices in Goodlettsville, Tennessee, we didn't get the usual rumors of the goings on. We heard about things after they had taken place. Even though Hal Smith had played fiddle on the *Barn Dance* for a short time in the forties, I feel like I can say that his main interest in the Valley was purely financial. Most of his business trips into the Valley were during the week, and when he was in on Saturday, he usually left before showtime. Hank Cochran took a back seat to the operation from the very beginning. One of the trips he did make was to attend his wedding to Miss Jeannie Seely. They chose the little Redbud Schoolhouse as the location for their wedding.

It might surprise you to learn that the most publicized wedding in Renfro Valley was not the Cochran-Seely wedding in the seventies, but that of country boy Coy Priddy and his pretty bride, Edith, on the stage of the Old Barn during the broadcast of a Saturday night *Barn Dance* in 1947. That made for quite a bit of entertainment for those in attendance. Bashful Coy not only had a little trouble with his lines but ended up placing the ring on Edith's thumb, which brought a tremendous amount of amusement to John Lair, who was trying to keep the radio listening audience filled in on what was going on. A recording of that broadcast is among a series of tapes we offer for sale in our little Down Memory Lane section.

On a much more serious occasion, *Jamboree* entertainer Carrie Stone said her "I dos" to her young man on stage of the Old Barn in 1992. Bun Wilson supplied the laughs that night by kissing the bride a few dozen times. Today, there are at least two or three weddings and sometimes more that take place in Renfro Village's little Freedom Church each year.

In the summer of 1969, the *Renfro Valley Barn Dance* and *Gatherin'* welcomed a new name to its list, Buster Bruner. He came to fill in for Glenn Thompson for a short while. Buster was an acquaintance of Bee Lucas and lived in the same area. The Bullock Sisters, Gwen and Linda Bullock, and Kathy Brown returned to the *Barn Dance* after a few years' absence. Buster Samples, a long-time friend and Jack-of-all-musical-trades, joined the show as my engineer assistant and part-time vocalist. It was Buster's voice that you heard on those WCKY broadcast recordings announcing, "It's Saturday night in Renfro Valley and time for the *Renfro Valley Barn Dance*."

I can't say I remember the first time I introduced a young Ernie Sowder to the *Barn Dance* audience, but that is understandable as we were, at the time, making available one or more spots on each show for guests. Unlike most of the others, however, Ernie was invited to stay on as a member of the show. He now shares one of the top three positions in seniority.

The Lodge Restaurant in the Valley was our main hangout; however, about this time Old Joe Clark and wife, Jean, leased the restaurant formerly known as Belly Acres, which was located on U.S. 25 in Renfro Valley about three-tenths of a mile south of Renfro Creek where Hardees' Restaurant now stands. Old Joe would run his early morning shift on WRVK, then go straight to the head table at the restaurant, where he would sit greeting customers while Jean did the work.

The Belly Acres Restaurant has been gone from the scene for a good many years, yet from time to time I keep the memory alive in one of my comedy routines. Even though Belly Acres Restaurant was located on the south side of Renfro Creek, it had a direct tie to the Renfro Valley entertainment years before Old Joe Clark took it over. It was the brainchild of fiddler and master of ceremonies Smokey Ward, or maybe it would be more correct to say it was the result of second thoughts by Smokey. Smokey had been invited to the unveiling of a new automobile that had caused quite a bit of excitement around the country. This new car was called the Tucker. Smokey became so caught up in the prospect of its success that he managed to swing a contract with the company for a dealership in little old Renfro Valley, Kentucky. As soon as he returned home, he set about buying the land and building the building that would be his office and showroom for the car of the future. Almost before the mortar was dry in the concrete block building, Tucker closed down and went out of business. For most this would have been their finish, but for Smokey Ward, this was just a minor set back. Smokey's decision to turn the building into a restaurant in Renfro Valley just around the curve from the big Lodge Restaurant brought on some bellyaching, which resulted in giving Smokey a name for his new business.

1970 to 1980

Confusion Reigns

By 1970 the stations carrying the *Gatherin'* had grown to eighty, more than doubling in just a year's time. Hal Smith's KOA campgrounds opened a half mile out of the Valley. It was evident that Renfro Valley was attracting some attention, as we were treated to occasional visits by some of the entertainers from other shows around the country.

Pee Wee King and Redd Stewart were long-time friends of the Valley and chose our Old Barn and locations around the Valley to film a portion of their movie *Petticoat Junction*. I don't know if Hank Cochran and Jeannie Seely spent the night in our honeymoon cabin, but I do know that Johnny Russell and his new bride came to spend their honeymoon there, as had Little Jimmie Dickens once upon a time.

Hal Smith and Pee Wee King announced plans for a new non-profit organization to be known as the Preservation of American Music Society, Inc., which was to be located here in Renfro Valley. The Society was to be directed by Pee Wee. It was planned that others would provide a rest home for aging country music performers and house a special museum to pay tribute to the pioneers of country music. This "old age home," as Old Joe Clark called it, never got beyond an artist's drawing, which hung on the wall of Wade Ray's office. Old Joe and I used to wonder out loud if our music might disqualify us from a place in that rest home. Neither of us ever dreamed that we would be around long enough that we would qualify as museum pieces!

From time to time we were treated to visits from old-timers who were former Renfro Valley entertainers. Reuben Powell and the Renfro Valley Tape Club invited some of the old-timers, including Doc Hopkins, Violet of the Coon Creek Girls, Linda Lou and Emory Mar-

Scene from JamArt Pictures, Inc., production of *Pee Wee King's Country Western Hoedown* filmed just outside the Old Barn by the old water tank that stood for about thirty years.

tin, Troy Gibbs, Ralph Grubbs, Miss Ruth, John Lair, and Coy Priddy, to a convention of the club.

This was my first meeting with Coy Priddy. Of course, I had heard about him, but you couldn't appreciate Coy until you had met him. He was a favorite of John Lair's. Later, when Coy returned to the Valley and Mr. Lair had grown too feeble to emcee the show, he always reserved the introduction of Coy Priddy for himself prior to his leaving the Barn to retire for the night. Coy was the countriest country boy that I ever met. His rendition of "Blue Moon of Kentucky" and his mandolin pickin' were so real that the audience would not let Coy leave the stage without an encore. Coy didn't drive; he traveled to Renfro Valley in the forties by Greyhound Bus from his home in Louisville. When Susan Tomes, also from Louisville, joined the Renfro Valley Folks in 1980, she saw to it that Coy had a first-class ride all the way in and back. Always looking out for Coy, she and he became the best of buddies.

The *Barn Dance* in the summer of 1970 had its third Bluegrass band consisting of four young men from nearby Jackson County— Billy and Bobby Gabbard and Harold and Hobert Russell. They became known as the Jackson County Boys. They later changed their billing to the Russell Brothers. Later, Hobert Russell dropped out and James Parker from the Parker Brothers Band took his place in the

Coy Priddy.

group. I was honored to have them record one of my songs, and I can truly say that I have never heard better harmony by any group than that of the Russell Brothers.

The *Barn Dance* was televised for the first time by Kentucky Educational Television in the summer of 1970 and was shown by a network of stations across the state. I can't help but wonder if that tape is still around someplace. The *Barn Dance* returned to radio by way of tape recordings of the program that were broadcast over some of the stations that carried the *Sunday Morning Gatherin'*. We had no sponsor for the *Renfro Valley Barn Dance* program, but we did offer for sale a family Bible. Grant Turner did the pitch on the Bible.

Horse shows and rodeos were making their way onto the special events calendar. I don't know just how successful they were, but they were bringing us some badly needed activity. A second annual *All-Night Sing* was added to the special events line-up. Doc Jack Lewis, family physician in nearby Mt. Vernon and steel guitar enthusiast, was sitting in more and more on our Renfro Valley shows. It was, or I should say it still is, a unique experience working the stage with your family doctor, but that's the way it's been for many of us for a long time in Renfro Valley.

Doc Lewis watched his first Renfro Valley show in his hometown of Hyden, Kentucky, when he was about nine or ten years old. He was already tinkering with the guitar; however, he became so impressed with one of the stars of the Renfro Valley show, Hawaiian guitarist Jerry Byrd, that he made up his mind then and there that he wanted to follow in Jerry's footsteps. I speak for so many when I say we're glad Mom and Pop Lewis first of all prevailed upon Jack to become a doctor of medicine.

As fate would have it, Jack's first practice was in Mt. Vernon, and Renfro Valley lay halfway between his home and the hospital where he practiced. Day in and day out he drove through Renfro Valley with never a thought of stopping, but one day on an impulse that he cannot even explain today, he did. Harold Flynn, who was playing steel guitar on the *Barn Dance* and the *Gatherin'* on a temporary basis, was there trying out a new guitar that he had just made for himself. Doc had never played or seen a pedal guitar played and was so taken with Harold's music that he bought that guitar right there on the spot and set out to learn to play it. I was around when that learning first began, and I want to tell you I was by Doc like John Lair was by Don Harper. I thought to myself, "There's a good set of golf clubs out there someplace that needs to be put to use." Doc has since become one of our best and hardest working musicians.

In 1993, when the *Jamboree* took on the new country format, I asked our owner, Warren Rosenthal, if he would like to add a saxophone to the band. He gave me the go-ahead to contact Doc, and we are proud he was able to join us as a regular member of the Straight Man Band. His practice was such that he could finish just about all the shows that he started, but there was a time when you might see Doc get up from his steel guitar right in the middle of a song, and you knew that there was a baby out there someplace wanting to be born. We've had an emergency or two in the audience when Doc came in mighty handy. Of course, we all tried to get free medical advice from time to time. Doc never flat-out refused, but once he started saying, "Go in there in the dressing room, take off your clothes, and I'll be there in a minute," the requests have slowed up a mite. At the beginning of our 1998 season, Doc's medical practice dictated that he leave the band, but I'll bet he will return somewhere down the road.

Robert Thompson, bass singer with the *Gatherin'* in the late sixties and seventies, was our first saxophone player. He was not a member of our *Barn Dance* Band, but we featured him on the *Barn Dance* for a couple of years. Bob was a local boy who had the honor of working with the Billy Vaughn Orchestra in his early career.

When Entertainment Corporation of America bought Renfro Valley, the entertainers and those of us who were full-time employees of Renfro Valley Folks really expected something of long-lasting importance to finally happen in the Valley where time had stood still for much too long. We weren't sure if we were going to like it or if we would even be a part of it. But, we reasoned, why would successful, professional, mainstream entertainers and businessmen obligate themselves to the operation of the place if they were not intending to move forward in some way or other? What we didn't consider or really know enough about to consider were the investors, their tax shelters, and how that works sometimes when nothing else does. Now I'm not saying that ECA didn't have some plans in the beginning. As I mentioned earlier, they rolled out a preview of an old age home, nursing home, retirement home that we could look forward to.

It wasn't too long until Hal Smith, who by this time had become sole owner, had (to use his own phrase) "soured on Renfro Valley, the *Barn Dance*, the entertainers, in fact, all of Rockcastle County."

I don't know what he could have had against the talent. Many of them barely knew who he was. I know he once told me, when I became manager of radio station WRVK, that a good manager never became too close to his employees. This was a preach that he seemed to practice. He once told me he regretted he hadn't fired everyone the first day he took charge. He became so upset with the local officials for not cooperating with him that he talked about dismantling every building in the Valley and moving them along with the *Barn Dance* and the *Gatherin'* to the Cave City area down close to Bowling Green.

I had never met Mr. Smith before he came into Renfro Valley, and ultimately I worked for him for a total of twenty years at the *Barn Dance* and the radio station, longer than I've ever worked for any one individual. Yet, I know very little more about him today than I did the first time I met him. One thing I do know is that he paid as agreed right down to the penny and gave each employee a full week's pay as a Christmas bonus. If he had to drive up from Nashville to see that the paychecks were not late, he did; that's important too.

It just seemed to me that almost from the very beginning, the *Barn Dance* was just kind of set adrift. We received very little attention or publicity other than when we shared the stage with one or more of the Nashville recording stars. If I had to guess why ECA failed to make it, and it's only a guess, I'd say it was their failure to recognize Renfro Valley's most valuable asset—our rich history of shows and talent. Succeeding owners put most of their attention on the *Barn Dance* and the *Jamboree*. They made some changes in talent, but they kept most of the entertainers who were in place at the time. Their biggest change, and the most important one, was in the talent that they added to the shows. They set about getting us as much publicity as possible from television and radio and personal appearances. And when we were a strong show, they built us the New Barn Theater and made the Old Barn more comfortable for our guests to enjoy the entertainment we had to offer. We still roll out the red carpet for the Nashville stars almost every week now, but we know the Renfro Valley performers are appreciated when we can look out in the audience and see certain seats occupied almost every show by Warren Rosenthal, current owner, and his wife, Betty. I can tell you right now that that is mighty important.

I will give ECA credit for one thing. They brought us Bun Wilson, though I will probably regret saying so. Bun first came to the show in 1966 as a guest. It didn't take long for Bun and I to become close friends, as we had a whole lot in common. We began planning the day when we would be able to work on stage together and not be held to two minutes. That opportunity came about twenty years later when we had a chance to do it our way on the new *Renfro Valley Jamboree* show.

When Bun joined the Renfro Valley show, he joined a long line of funny folks that have come in all shapes and sizes—tall and short, extra tall and short, fat and skinny, old and young, male and female, and now sober and otherwise. Their styles have been just as varied. Some specialize in visual comedy while others have featured monologues. Some were pretty good vocalists, a few were excellent musicians, some worked as a team while others preferred to go it alone. From the Renfro Valley stage the laugh-makers have always had the best audience that they could ever ask for. The atmosphere behind the scenes has most always been just as favorable. While other shows its size might feature one or two comedian stars, the *Barn Dance* presented three, four, and sometimes more. One year after opening night the number was up to eight, probably the most there's ever been at any one time. While others depended on the recording stars to carry the show, over the years this responsibility fell to the comedians and to the novelty acts at Renfro Valley. There's an old show poster in

Bun Wilson, Betty Lou York, and Pete Stamper.

existence that promoted top billing to four comedians and a novelty band over one, lone female vocalist.

Slim Miller would have to be considered the first comic of the *Barn Dance*. The team of A'nt Idy and Little Clifford was its most publicized. This act was comprised of a woman character actor from the Weaver Brothers Vaudeville Show and a local boy, Harry Mullins. Later they became a trio when Danny Duncan joined them as Uncle Junie. Two of the four founders of the *Renfro Valley Barn Dance* were comics, Clyde "Red" Foley and Whitey Ford. If for national recognition the names of all the comedians were compared to all the other Renfro Valley acts, it most surely would have gone to the comics. The untimely death of A'nt Idy kept her fame confined mainly to the *Barn Dance* audience, but the others became well known throughout the

Little Eller Long and Shorty Hobbs.

country, including the Duke of Paducah, Gabe Tucker, Shug Fisher, Little Eller and Homer and Jethro, just to name a few. Others you might remember on the *Barn Dance* stage were Granny Harper, Gene "Nubbin" Cobb, Abner and Fanny, Sy, Shorty Hobbs, Barefoot Brownie, Herschel Collins, James "Goober" Buchanan, Luke "Warmwater" McNeily, Brother, Charlie Harrison, Jack and Maude Salisbury, Clarence and Waldo, Jerry Isaacs (the Chicken Man) and, of course, Old Joe Clark, Bun Wilson, Betty Lou York, and yours truly.

In addition to the comedy you'll find on our *Barn Dance* and *Jamboree* shows, Bun, Betty and I have been getting together each Satur-

Bun Wilson, Pete Stamper, and James "Goober" Buchanan.

day afternoon during the height of the season to do a thirty-five- to forty-five-minute comedy show with a variety of routines, acts, and skits. So, I believe you can see we still take our comedy serious in Renfro Valley.

Now I don't mean to indicate that there was no activity from ECA during their management years. There were Appaloosa horse shows, rodeos, antique car shows, and the Bluegrass Festival. During their first five years there was quite a bit, but it all seemed to come from the outside and only a little of it stuck. Mac Wiseman produced our first Bluegrass Festival in July 1971, and I'm proud to say that it's still going strong. It's now called the Old Joe Clark Bluegrass Festival, but it's the one and the same that began twenty-eight years ago.

An event that had a little success but not enough to stand on its own was the Fiddlers' Convention. After two or three years it was combined with the Bluegrass Festival, and soon it was dropped altogether. However, it was revived as a separate event in the eighties under the direction of Jim Gaskin and is now one of our biggest and

Bun Wilson, Don Warden, Pete Stamper, and Curt Caldwell.

fastest-growing events. Maybe time doesn't always stand still in Renfro Valley.

Before 1971 was up, Mr. Lair returned as editor of the *Bugle* and once again took command of the *Gatherin'* and the *Barn Dance*. We now know that he had decided to buy the Valley back if possible and would have left no stone unturned in pursuit of that goal. The parking lots were full on Saturday nights and Sunday mornings; the *Gatherin'* was now just short of one hundred stations, and the Saturday night *Barn Dance* was again on the air. At age seventy-seven, John Lair was once more trying to get back home to Renfro Valley. But he would have a long way to go before he could again say that he had made it.

When Mr. Lair broke ranks with ECA in 1968 we didn't expect to see him back. But Renfro Valley was still his first love, and he set out to get it back one way or the other. And he did. He lived to be ninety-one years of age. It's my opinion, had he not been able to regain ownership of the venue, he would not have fared that well. I think others who were around and saw him on a daily basis will agree that his

Pete Stamper, Virginia Sutton, and Goober Buchanan.

Old Joe Clark.

decline, or at least the appearance of failing health, began to show on him. He moved more slowly and would seem to be preoccupied and depressed for the first time in his life.

I did not have knowledge of the communication between Mr. Lair and Mr. Smith. I can't say which one made the first move that brought John back into the picture. What I can safely say, I believe, is he sure as shootin' did not come back just for the opportunity of working for the new owner of Renfro Valley. I have an idea he thought that if he was going to buy the place once again, he needed to be on the inside. And, of course, it didn't hurt to have access to the Renfro Valley *Sunday Morning Gatherin'* and the *Bugle* to publicize some of the activity that he had going over at his saltpeter cave.

Salt Peter Cave is located just a few short miles from Renfro Valley as the crow flies but a far piece by the narrow winding road you must take to get to it. It lay dormant most of the years I have been acquainted with it. Most of those years John shared ownership with a local doctor and then his widow. When he finally bought her interest, John tried unsuccessfully to develop the cave and surrounding area. It was sold a few years ago to an organization dedicated to its preservation. Its history is noted in John Lair's "History of Rockcastle County."

As I have indicated before, these were very confusing and frustrating times for the employees. We were working for an absentee owner under the management of the founder, who was dead set on becoming the owner again, and directed by Glen Pennington, another who harbored a desire to claim the Valley for himself. But good entertainers never let a little thing like chaos keep them from entertaining their audience and having fun while doing it. You could say our shows were free-wheeling and a little undisciplined at times, but I think some of our best entertainment came out of this period.

The management team of Smith, Lair, and Pennington was doomed from the beginning, but it did last for one more season before once again John dropped out, this time taking the Pioneer Museum with him. It had been operated by ECA on a leased basis, as it was not included in the sale. Ralph Marcum returned as editor of the *Bugle,* and Glen Pennington continued to emcee the *Barn Dance.* We went back to replays of the *Gatherin'* on the air, and I took over again with the live portions on Sunday morning.

It wasn't long after that until a bulldozer showed up early one morning across the road from the Old Country Store and started moving dirt on a piece of land that John Lair owned. After a couple of days up went a big billboard that read, "Coming Soon. John Lair's all-new *Country Music Show*." Now, although John Lair's name is not on the deed or even mentioned on the day that show was born, he was the daddy of the *New Jamboree* just as sure as shootin'. I've always said that I believe before the ink was dry on the contract to sell Renfro Valley, he was regretting his decision. Well, when that sign went up, those of us who knew Mr. Lair had our doubts as to the seriousness of it. First, the word "new" and John Lair just didn't fit together very well. Most of all, we knew that he would never be satisfied in any new barn as long as the old one was standing just a few yards away.

His partner in this venture was a builder and developer by the name of Joe Haney. Now, John Lair was known as a super salesman, but this time he did a better job than he really intended to do. This bluff really surprised only one person, and that was Haney. When he found out that John had no intention of building a barn or anything else on this spot of land, it was too late. Haney was already sold on the idea. He just went down the road a little way, leased some land, and built the barn himself. Soon the footlights went up on Joe Haney's *Renfro Valley Jamboree*.

The building of this new barn would bring about some events that would affect us all on down the line. The new red barn was the first competition the *Renfro Valley Barn Dance* had ever had. Whatever plans Hal Smith had for the *Barn Dance* were altered somewhat by this new competition. Just how much competition it was in ticket sales I really don't know. The talent of the two shows had sort of a friendly battle going, although we never really got acquainted with our neighbors as the shows were performed pretty much at the same time.

Glittering lights went up on the end of the new red barn and a loud speaker was placed up in the eave, and the music that came from that speaker was an attention-getter. Now, on our side of the road we had WRVK radio station. We didn't leave it to the chance that our guests were tuned to 1460 on the radio dial, we made sure they heard what was going on. We placed the biggest bullhorn we could find up on the side of the Museum Building and aimed it at the big red barn across the road. Folks might not have been able to see the battle of the barns, but they sure heard it. Their volume came up, ours came up, theirs came up, ours came up.

The entertainers were just having fun. But behind the scenes there was some serious maneuvering going on. And it was confusing to folks to suddenly find two shows on properties that were not commonly owned, each with separate ticket offices. They had assumed it was all in the family. Whether Mr. Smith really felt threatened by this new competition, I don't know, but he used the confusion as an excuse to secretly try to buy out the red barn. According to Smith, Glen Pennington was sent across the road to act as his agent and to find out if he could purchase Joe Haney's *Renfro Valley Jamboree*. But, acting on his own behalf, Glen bought the show for himself! I heard recently that he gave a used Cadillac and $10,000. This brought about court action between Mr. Smith and Pennington, Smith claiming that Pennington acted on his own when he should have been representing the company. Smith lost this battle in the Mt. Vernon courts.

Well, this new show under the guidance of Glen Pennington was something else altogether. Unlike Joe Haney, Glen Pennington had the know-how and the financial backing. But, more important, he had an undying interest in Renfro Valley.

The *Barn Dance* had recently closed for the winter months for the very first time. There had been quite a bit of concern as to whether we could get back under way in the spring or not, how we could educate the guests to the fact that we were not closing for good. If there was any difficulty that spring, I never knew it. I know some of us welcomed the break, but some of the *Barn Dance* talent just wanted a change of scenery, so it seemed.

"Alfie" Smith, owner of the Renfro Valley Lodge, decided he would take advantage of the shut-down and had a little Saturday night pickin' and singin' session in the big dining room over at the Lodge. He hired some of the idled *Renfro Valley Barn Dance* talent for this shindig. This went against the wishes of Hal Smith, and when the new season rolled around it led to the dismissal of this talent from the *Barn Dance*.

With John Lair and Glen Pennington both out of the picture, I began to take added responsibility at the *Barn Dance*. I served as entertainment director (without title) in addition to doing the *Gatherin'* on Sunday morning and sharing the emcee work on the *Barn Dance* with Al Ballinger. As it turned out, this continued to be a learning time for me.

For some unknown reason, Ralph Marcum left the *Bugle* and the job was given to Bill Williams, who, as far as I know, had no interest and probably very little knowledge as to what Renfro Valley was all about. As with our absentee owner, Bill was an absentee editor. The

Musicians on stage: "Doc" Jack Lewis, Terry Clark, Old Joe Clark, and Jim Gaskin.

slogan, "If a man tooteth not his own horn, the same is tooteth not" was dropped from the *Renfro Valley Bugle* heading. And under this new editor, the Renfro Valley horn stopped blowing for quite some time.

The subject matter of the *Bugle* stories ran from the life of Jesse James and Belle Starr to the Hollywood stars Tim McCoy and John Wayne. Even sax player Ace Cannon and his battle with the bottle was a big feature. Months went by without barely a mention of the *Renfro Valley Barn Dance*, much less the *Barn Dance* talent. An unknown Johnny Cash impersonator from Oklahoma got a feature story but not the *Barn Dance* talent. The paper might as well have been produced in the heart of New York City or Hollywood for all the good it did for Renfro Valley. Oh, I guess it was interesting reading for nostalgia buffs in general, but it did very little to sell our product—good family entertainment from Renfro Valley.

Some new talent came on the *Barn Dance* during 1972: Bob Roark, a former WHAS radio vocalist; Cliff Cochran, a young Nashville, Tennessee, recording artist; Charlie Harrison, vocalist and comic from our neighboring county of Laurel. Brenda Ball made a guest appearance on the *Barn Dance* on her way to the *Jamboree* stage as a regular. Bluegrass mandolin player/vocalist Dean Huddleston joined us.

It was about this same time that the *Renfro Valley Barn Dance* had its first what you would call staff band as we know a staff band today. It included Bonnie Whitaker, guitarist; Glenn Thompson, lead guitar; J.C. Sawyer playing steel guitar; his brother, Elmer Sawyer, on the bass fiddle; Terry Benge, keyboard; and Renfro Valley's first full-fledged drummer, Bob Tony.

Bonnie's daughter, Mary Lou, was a feature on the *Barn Dance* for a while, and then she along with her Elvis (husband, J. Perkins) made their way to the *Jamboree* staff as regulars. A good part of this band, along with Doc Lewis, would end up on the staff of the *Renfro Valley Jamboree.*

Renfro Valley was split three ways—Hal Smith, owner of the *Barn Dance;* Alfie Smith, owner of the Renfro Valley Lodge and Motel; and Glen Pennington, the new proprietor of the *Renfro Valley Jamboree.* The only one left out was John Lair, founder of the whole shebang. But not for long! Behind the scenes, John Lair, Glen Pennington, and Alfie Smith had formed a pact to buy out Hal Smith, who, by this time I suppose, had seen the handwriting on the wall and would agree to sell his side of the road to this new organization. This would, for the first time in many years, put the *Barn Dance*, the Renfro Valley Lodge and Motel, and the new show, the *Renfro Valley Jamboree*, all under one common ownership. But this wasn't going to work either. As in the beginning, John Lair, even at the age of eighty-two, wanted it all to himself.

Back in the Saddle Again

In January 1975, I left Renfro Valley for my second time. I was given an honor that comes to very few in their careers. I was invited to travel a few months with the prettiest, most talented, and most popular female star in all of show business, Dolly Parton, and her Traveling Family Band. I have quite a few memories from those months, but the one I'll record here was the day when Dolly and Renfro Valley and I all came together for the first time. While I was on the road with her I kept my home here in nearby Mt. Vernon. Even though I continued to work for Renfro Valley Folks on the *Gatherin'* production and the *Barn Dance* now and then, I lost out on what was going on in the Valley as far as special events were concerned. I was only home two days a week. I usually headed out for Nashville on Thursday and boarded Dolly's bus for the trip to our dates. Sunday nights or Monday mornings I usually drove back home. This was about 400 miles of driving a week.

One week in May 1975, we had only one show booked and that was in Paintsville, Kentucky, on a Saturday night. Paintsville lay northeast of Renfro Valley a few miles. If Dolly would agree to pick me up in Renfro Valley, it would save me a lot of time and miles to and from Nashville. In order to do this, her bus would have to travel about twenty to thirty miles on a winding, narrow, two-lane road. But in spite of this, she agreed. I should have left well enough alone, but I couldn't help but think what a surprise it would be for my disc jockey buddy Al Balinger and the WRVK listening audience if she would stop in at the station down in the Valley for a short interview. I asked, and again she said yes—but under one condition. We'd be running

Wayne Hensley, Allen Hensley, Diedre Collinsworth, Roy Martin, Charlie Napier, Dolly Parton, Virginia Sutton at WRVK in 1975.

late, she said, so I had to promise her that I would not let it be known that she was going to be there. I had already assured her that at that time of day there would be absolutely no one except the disk jockey and two or three office personnel in the Valley. I crossed my heart and hoped to die if I told anyone. This was the way I wanted it to be anyway because I couldn't wait to see the look on Al's face when Miss Dolly Parton walked into the studio.

Saturday morning found me in good spirits. Most everyone around the country had already heard that I was working for Dolly, but this was going to clinch it. The ones who were not listening at the time she was on would surely hear about it later, because I knew Al would be talking about it all weekend and longer. I grabbed my show clothes and headed for the Valley. I wanted to be there in plenty of time in case the bus was running ahead of schedule. I may have been smiling as I entered the Valley, anticipating the look I was soon to see on my buddy Al's face. The look I had on my face when the smile faded is anybody's guess. As my granddaughter Christina would say, "I was like—What in tarnation!" There were people everywhere I looked, cars, trucks, pick-up trucks by the dozens. I had never seen this many people in Renfro Valley at 11:00 A.M. on a Saturday morning in my life. I couldn't help but notice that many of them were local folks, and I quickly realized that this was not a *Barn Dance* crowd. Only one thing I figured could have brought them all out—somehow or other they had learned that Dolly was coming. Who could have told them? Somewhere between the place I parked my car and the radio station I learned the truth. My secret was still safe. These folks from five counties around were there to take part in a Cass Walker Coon Dog Trade and Sale Day. The relief I felt was short-lived, however; my next question was, What is Dolly going to think? I decided I'd better go up the road a ways to meet the bus so she wouldn't have time to do too much thinkin' before I had a chance to explain.

I got to the bridge that crossed Renfro Creek just as the bus arrived. When the bus stopped and I stepped on and looked at my pretty boss, I knew I had not made it in time. I could tell that she thought I had surely betrayed her. I was quick to assure her I had not. But then having to tell Dolly Parton that the crowd was there to see Cass Walker's Coon Dogs and Flea Market and not her came off quite a bit short of funny. Like the song says, "Sometimes you just can't win."

Later that year, the merchants and citizens of Rockcastle County got together to honor a favorite son. A little outdoor theater was set up under the trees about where the entrance to the new barn concession is now located. The portable stage used for the Bluegrass Festival was moved to that location, decorated with red, white, and blue crepe paper in celebration of the Fourth of July as well as John Lair's birthday. A couple of mikes, a podium, and chairs for Mr. and Mrs. Lair and honored guests were added, and I served as the emcee of "This Is Your Life, John Lair Day." I didn't have to reach back in my memory for details of this event because Ruben Powell, founder of the Renfro Valley Tape Club, had his recorder going and captured every minute.

John's long-time friends, Colonel Harlan Sanders, Reverend and Mrs. Ford Philpot, Emory and Linda Lou Martin, Old Joe Clark, Glen Pennington, Lily May and the Coon Creek Girls, Smokey Ward, Betty Callahan, Betty Foley and Virginia Sutton were all in attendance, and

I suppose most important as far as musical history was concerned was the presence of Bradley Kincaid and Doc Hopkins. I revisited that tape recording not long ago, hearing how we spoke about the past and honored Mr. Lair for the things that he had done. I couldn't help but wonder if, as he sat on that stage and enjoyed this few minutes in the spotlight, he knew then he was just months away from the ownership of Renfro Valley once again.

I don't think the feeling we had over another change of the guard at Renfro Valley could really be called excitement. But I believe we all felt good just knowing that at least something was going to take place. I think the true feeling was maybe more of a ho-hum attitude. By this time I think we were all resigned to the notion that Renfro Valley was never to be anything more than just a place in history.

The *new* man at the wheel was eighty-two-year-old John Lair. So, if nothing else, at least he could leave this world with everything he ever wanted—his Renfro Valley home. If there was any spark of hope in any of us that something might be done, it lay in the fact that one of John's new partners was Glen Pennington. We knew Glen would not be involved if he didn't mean business in one way or the other.

Lodge owner Alfie Smith, the third partner in this unlikely trio, could not be counted on for any meaningful advancement of the show part of this business, as this was entirely out of his line. Well, I had better not say entirely. He was a showman of sorts, sort of on a personal basis. Alfie was a short, stocky gentleman who dressed more in the style of a Chicago mob boss than a Kentucky Colonel. He wore dark, tailor-made suits, diamonds as big as hen eggs on his fingers, a tie, stickpin, gold-headed walking cane, and a big cigar. This was the way Alfie presented himself to his guests at the Lodge. Alfie's winning personality and boarding house-style dinners brought more success to the Lodge and the motel than they had ever seen before.

But I couldn't write any meaningful story about the Valley without a mention of Alfie Smith's son-in-law and daughter, Mr. and Mrs. Willard Collingsworth, and the old country store. The Renfro Valley Country Store became a part of the Renfro Valley settlement in late 1949 or early 1950. It was a vital part of the John Lair dream and the setting of a number of daily broadcasts on the CBS network called *The Country Store Program*. A broadcast studio was built in the back for this purpose. Would you believe tapes of some of those shows are still available at our Country Music Store! The original country store was furnished with the old cracker barrels, bolts of ribbons and remnants, a few overalls, work shoes, plaid shirts, a select line of canned goods, and some products that carried the label of our sponsor, General Foods. And there was the old cash register that used marbles for keeping track of the number of transactions. When a quarter, dime, nickel, dollar, whatever was taken in, a marble was placed in a certain compartment in the money drawer and at the end of the day you would count your marbles and know how much money you were supposed to have. At the end of the day, if the marbles and the money didn't jibe, it would be said, "He has lost his marbles." Now you know the origin of the expression.

To listen to one of the programs you would think there was someone sitting around the Old Country Store's pot-bellied stove just about all the time and that the store itself was a beehive of activity, when in truth this was not so. If it had not been for the fact that the post office was located in the store, there would hardly have been any traffic at all except maybe on Saturdays. When the radio programs were closed, so was the life at the country store. After a few years the store moved to the old Main Street location, and the store building and studio were closed. It opened for a while as a craft shop, then closed again and remained closed until Alfie talked his son-in-law and daughter into taking a gamble, quitting their jobs in northeastern Kentucky, coming to Renfro Valley, and opening it up once more. Willard once told me that he had absolutely no faith that this would work but Alfie seemed to believe it could so he went along. I suppose Alfie knew Willard better than Willard knew himself.

The Collingsworths stocked this little store more like a rural store was operated in this day and time; they opened early in the morning and stayed late at night, sometimes on Saturday nights at least until midnight. And this was seven days a week. They stocked to meet the daily demands of the community residents and the tourists alike. But the most valuable fixture was Willard himself. Willard never met a stranger, and if he did he didn't stay that way long. The fact of the matter is, Willard became better known to some of our guests than many of our entertainers. Willard loved to meet and greet people and went out of his way to order special tapes, records, special souvenirs, hard-to-get wearing apparel, and Farmer Brown's country hams. He would take their orders and ship them anywhere in the country. Folks planned their trips to Renfro Valley to give them enough time to spend a while at Willard's.

He told me that when he first came into the Valley they had a meeting with Alfie and John Lair and discussed how the store would be operated. One of the questions that came up was what he would call it. John suggested that he would do better business if he called it the Renfro Valley Country Store, the name that it had carried since its beginning. Willard agreed that this was a good idea, but it wasn't too long until most of the public was referring to this location as "Willard's." It was down to Willard's for this or down to Willard's for that. Let me tell you that this success did not go unnoticed by John Lair. He was more than just a little bit envious of this young whipper snapper who was making money hand over fist at a so-called country store when he had given the public the real thing and couldn't make it work.

Willard's store wasn't a museum piece, but it was old-fashioned enough to interest the tourists and up-to-date enough to meet the demands of the local folks. Willard only advertised about once a year and that was at Christmastime. He would run a special on fruit and candy and let it be known by way of our little radio station. He also held a drawing for a holiday basket. He would prepare two big baskets loaded down with apples, oranges, tangerines, a variety of candy, nuts of all kinds, and a great big Farmer Brown's country ham. One basket was for the holder of the lucky ticket from a free registration, and one basket was for the disc jockey who would bring the equipment down to the store just before sign-off on Christmas Eve for a live drawing. He would also throw in a special box of chocolates for my wife, Minnie Lee, because he knew that I was going to manage somehow or other to be lucky enough to be that disc jockey.

I never thought I would ever see a business in Renfro Valley any more successful than Willard's, but I have, and once again it's the same old country store building. It is now home to our Renfro Valley Country Music Store, and our Willard is pretty Miss Terry Jones, who is just as friendly and accommodating to her customers as Willard was.

At long last I had decided that Renfro Valley would be my home whatever took place, so I took advantage of an offer of a little farm in the Valley made by my good friend Sam Ford of Ford Brothers Realty and Auction Company. It had been part of the property where the KOA Campground was located and owned by J. Hal Smith, although not included in the Renfro Valley sale. All John Lair and his partners bought was the piece of property that they had previously owned, including the WRVK radio station. At the time Virginia Sutton was station manager, but she had decided to resign before the new owners would take over. A sale of a radio station must be approved by the

FCC, which was certain in this case, but no shortcuts could be taken. Sales pending announcements were being made in the newspaper and on the air at various times and intervals as required by the FCC, until they made the sale official. As a disc jockey at the station, where I had worked for the past eleven years, I was in the right place and at the right time to take over as acting manager for a month or so before the station changed hands.

One morning I got an urgent call from Hal telling me to pull all the station's sales announcements off the air immediately, that he was going to keep WRVK. Well, this was surprising news to me considering that John had always considered WRVK an important part of Renfro Valley and had been the one to put it on the air in the first place. I later learned a little of what took place. It seems that Mr. Lair wanted to move the tower and studio building off leased property on the south side of Renfro Valley Creek to the property on the north side just opposite where the tower was standing. This was going to cost in the neighborhood of $10,000 he was told, and I heard Glen and Alfie were not for the idea, at least not enough to help with the expense. I really can't say if John was getting the station back for himself or if this, too, was to be a three-way partnership. I never asked, and I see no reason to go to the trouble of trying to find out now, but there is the possibility that all three of these principal players looked at the radio station as a white elephant. Possibly, Mr. Lair was getting it back for himself only for sentimental reasons. As I mentioned earlier, the station had always furnished a couple or three of us with pretty good jobs over the years, but as a business, it never was much of a profit maker.

Hal Smith and Hank Cochran had bought the station for around $26,000 and in the years they owned it had made a few improvements, a new board and a couple or three tape machines. I understand Hal was letting Mr. Lair have it back for the price they paid. I never could understand why moving the tower to the Renfro Valley side of the road was such an important thing, as the lease was very reasonable, and, as far as I know, long-term. We do know that John Lair was set on getting the Valley back into 100 percent ownership somehow, somewhere along the line.

The other side of Renfro Valley Creek played a big part in these plans. We now know that he made an attempt to purchase that property a little later on, but did he have that in mind at the time the station became a problem? Could it be he planned to use the other

143

side of the road as leverage to gain full control of Renfro Valley? Would owning a radio station with a tower and transmitter on one side of the creek and a studio on the other have caused him problems when this plan was put into play? I only speculate on this now to show you the irony of it just a little bit later. But, any way you go about it, giving back the station was a costly decision. This cost John in two ways. Renfro Valley lost a good, little radio station, and it cost his heirs a few thousand dollars.

As I was already in place, as they say, Hal kept me on as station manager. We continued to operate out of the studio building there in the Valley for a while and then moved to a new location, a little building between the KOA campground and my newly acquired farm. We continued to use the tower and transmitter in its old location on the south side of Renfro Valley Creek on leased property until that property was purchased by John Lair, who ordered us out by the 31st of December 1979.

With the help of the sales talents of Country Charlie Napier, Miss Karen Noe, and Jim Gaskin, we almost doubled the station's income over the next six or seven years. In fact, just ten years after Mr. Lair's decision not to spend $26,000 for WRVK, the little station sold for $200,000. About halfway through this ten-year period, I leased the station with the option to buy for $110,000 and would have followed through on it had it not been for the fact that I was also tied to a deal for the KOA Campground. Hal wouldn't let me out of one without the other, and I couldn't make the campground work.

If any one of the players, including myself, had read the lease for the property where the station and transmitter building were located and paid attention, history would have been changed somewhere along the line. This lease had been in effect I suppose since 1957, just renewed every so often. It included a clause that said the station owner, after a specific amount of time, could buy the location where the tower and transmitter were located, which was bordered by the creek on the north side, U.S. 25 on the west, quite a few feet of property, for just $2,500. The question of moving the tower for $10,000 would never have come up. John Lair would have followed through with his purchase of WRVK or, if discovered at a later date, WRVK studios would have moved over by the tower on Renfro Creek rather than the KOA Campground hill.

You can always look back and see how things could have been changed, how they might have been made better. In fact, as I look back now, I realize things were better in the Valley in the late seventies than they had been for a long time. I'm not sure if we entertainers were that much aware of it then, but, as I mentioned before, we made our living in various ways through the week, and we'd come together on a Saturday night to have fun and give fun in the good times and the bad. That's why our guests to the *Barn Dance* always got just exactly what they came for. We always tried to make our entertainment the best we had to offer, regardless of what was going on in the wings.

Things were better for a number of reasons. The ECA years had brought the Valley to the attention of some important country music organizations in Nashville, and there had been a steady increase in visitors to the Valley. The country music industry had begun to shake off the effects that rock music had had on it in the late fifties and sixties just as Renfro Valley had felt the effects of the hard times and was now beginning to share in the better times. Even though our shows had been entertaining, I did mention earlier that they had for a little while been sort of on the loose side. Now they were being put back in line by Mr. Lair and Glen Pennington. Glen was holding down the fort over across the road at the *Jamboree* in the Red Barn, and John had control of the *Barn Dance* once more. I felt sorry for some of the band members who received the brunt of John's wrath on his first Saturday back on the job, finding more microphones and amplifiers on the Old Barn stage than he thought should be there. Our very fine steel player took it personally and left the show. Not only was Bob England a fine musician, he was and is a fine person. Too bad he and John didn't get a chance to work together; they would have hit it off just fine.

John wasted no time in announcing new plans for the future, but, as in the past, they seldom were accomplished for one reason or another. Up until Mr. Smith put in a KOA Campground about eight-tenths of a mile up the road from the Old Barn, campers had parked along the edges of the parking lot around the barns. This suited them fine, as they could pull in, back in, set up, lock up, see the show, visit the restaurant and Willard's, and never move until it was time to go home. When the KOA Campground opened, this became a no no. As long as there had been no other alternative, I suppose the health department had, let's say, looked the other way a little. But now, all of a sudden, they began to enforce the rules and would not let campers stay beyond a certain time after the show was over.

When Mr. Smith owned both the show and KOA Campground, this became a touchy situation. A $10 or $12 fee was charged at the campground, where $1 had been the fee for around the Barn parking if they used any electricity—otherwise it was free! It wasn't the money the guests objected to as much as the inconvenience. And many guests were upset when they found that they could no longer park at the Barn. Some did think that this was just to get the campground parking fee, but the truth was the health department was making the rules and strongly enforcing them. We'd played host to one of the big camping clubs on an annual basis until they were denied space at the Barn one year. I'm happy to say that, after many years absence, that club, along with a number of others, have found their way back to Renfro Valley, where they can now enjoy fine entertainment, stay in a first-class campground built in 1995, and be just a few steps from both the Old Barn and the New. This campground is a great addition to the Valley, as it helps the ticket sales for our Wednesday and Thursday night shows in addition to weekend sales.

It would have been a great move on Mr. Lair's part had he followed through with the plan or something similar twenty years ago. That was in the plans early in 1977. Camp hookups were to be installed around the edge of the parking lot that year. Far from being a campground, but it would have served to remedy a problem that had persisted until recently.

Another plan for that year, according to Mr. Lair, was the creation of another pioneer life museum, which made me wonder if a couple years earlier he had found himself in one of those Catch 22s. The *Renfro Valley Barn Dance* years earlier had made it possible for him to put together a fantastic pioneer museum. Later when he sold the *Barn Dance* he kept the museum. Did he then find himself having to sell the museum in order to buy back his *Barn Dance*? Another idea he promised to get off the ground that year was a Renfro Valley Hall of Fame. Actually, none of these projects really stood a chance of getting off the drawing board so long as there was a partner or two hanging around. John was not going to do anything that he would have to share with partners he intended to shuck as soon as possible.

I remember a couple of years later I came up with the idea of selling cassette recordings of the old *Gatherin's* that we had on file. I told him I thought there would be a big demand for them. He said, "You really think so?" I told him that I had had some folks asking about them and that we could offer them for sale on Sunday morning and advertise them in the *Bugle*. Then, sort of as if he was thinking out loud, he said, "Well, let's see, I'd have to share the profits out of

Coon Creek Girls in 1979: Kelli Cummins, Vicki Simmons, Betty Lin, Jan Cummins.

this with the folks across the road, wouldn't I?" And then to me he said, "Let's wait on that a while." He might have agreed had it been for anything other than the *Gatherin'*. I'm sure he looked at this Renfro Valley *Sunday Morning Gatherin'* as his own special creation and something he wouldn't want to share at all. Later, when John's daughter, Ann, took over operation of the Valley, she gave me the go-ahead on this project. It proved then to be a profitable enterprise and continues to be so today.

A young and pretty banjo-pickin' teenager joined the *Barn Dance*. She would win the admiration of Mr. Lair in a way no one had since Lily May. She was home folks, growing up just up the road a piece. Her mother and her mother's brothers had all worked at the Lodge or around the Old Barn when they were young. She, and later her sister, Kelli, would settle in as regular features on not only the *Barn Dance* but on the *Gatherin'* as well. She was Jan Cummins.

It was her coming to the Valley when she did that led to the formation of the New Coon Creek Girls: Jan and Kelli on banjo and guitar, along with a fiddler from Indiana who was already on the *Barn Dance*, Betty Lin. Just one other spot needed to be filled. For this they could not have made a better choice than another young lady from nearby Berea, Miss Vicki Simmons, bass player and vocalist. Her talent as a leader soon came shining through when Jan decided to drop out. Vicki took command of the group and later ownership of this all-girl Bluegrass band and fulfilled her responsibility for finding replacements for Jan, Kelli, and Betty as one by one they dropped out. The New Coon Creek Girls were one of the Bluegrass world's most colorful acts, holding down a regular spot on our *Renfro Valley Barn Dance* each Saturday night and as special acts on a variety of other shows. Like Bill Monroe's band, they have had a number of members that have come and gone over the years.

A member or two from the Porter Wagoner all-girl group and Wild Rose found their way to the Coon Creek Girls. The band has included (in order of their appearance) Jan Cummins (banjo), Betty Lin (fiddle), Kelli Cummins (guitar), Vicki Simmons (bass), Wanda Barnett (fiddle/guitar), Cathy Lavendar (guitar), Pam Gadd (banjo), Pam Perry (mandolin), Annie Kaser (banjo), Deanie Richardson (fiddle), Carmella Ramsey (fiddle), Ramona Church (banjo), Phylis Jones (guitar), Jennifer Wrinkle (fiddle), Dale Ann Bradley (guitar), Michelle Birkby (fiddle), Kathy Kuhn (fiddle), Kati Penn (fiddle). Pam Perry worked 1985–88 and came back in 1992 for three more years. At this writing the New Coon Creek Girls have disbanded for the first time in the nineteen-year history. Dale Ann Bradley has formed a new group under the name of Dale Ann Bradley and Coon Creek.

Declining Years of John Lair

Ralph Gabbard, Berea native and the country's youngest general manager of a major TV station, WKYT-TV in Lexington, was showing an interest in Renfro Valley again in August 1977. I say again, as he had earlier as a teenager picked up some of his broadcasting education at our little WRVK radio station, and later as a television producer he filmed the first video of the Renfro Valley *Sunday Morning Gatherin'*. He was now producing a TV show that included a portion of the *Barn Dance* and *Gatherin'*, including an interview with John Lair hosted by songwriter-entertainer John Ireson, an occasional performer on the *Renfro Valley Barn Dance*. The only thing that makes this worth mentioning right here is that Ralph continued to pop up from time to time in Renfro Valley, as did Glen Pennington. What would really make the difference is when they popped up together in 1989, a dozen years or so on down the road.

Coy Priddy was now back on the *Barn Dance* after a long, long absence. Joining the *Barn Dance* and the *Sunday Morning Gatherin'* were the Jubilee Four. Arliss and Pauline Harris, Elmer and Peggy Bentley, and son, Phillip, made up this fine gospel quartet from nearby Laurel County. And Miss Jeanne Gibson, a young lady who had won the admiration of John Lair when we made our movie in 1965, came back for a couple of seasons. Jeanne was "small in stature but with a big voice." John Lair used to just love to introduce her to the *Renfro Valley Barn Dance* audience. In addition to considering her one of the finest vocalists who had come along, he enjoyed telling the audience about how she made her living when she was younger, growing up

149

and paying her way through school. She was a bulldozer operator and became one of Kentucky's fine schoolteachers.

It was kind of like old times in 1977 for Mr. Lair; he had his Barn Dance back, and old-timers were joining the show—Jeanne, Coy, Troy Gibbs. Patty Flye would soon be making her move back. But then he lost the most important one in his life, the one and only partner he never wanted to lose. The death of his wife, Virginia Crawford Lair, left a vacancy he couldn't replace.

Then on March 1, 1978, less than two years after becoming a partner in the *Renfro Valley Barn Dance*, Alfie Smith died. He had made a mark on this little settlement during the eighteen years his family had operated the Lodge Restaurant and Motel. His place in the new organization, at his request, went to his young son, Gary. Mr. Lair's daughter, Jenny Lee King, took over the editing chores at the *Bugle* newspaper. Our horn was tooting "Renfro Valley" again.

Vernon Rainwater, one of the best male vocalists to come Renfro Valley's way in a long, long time, joined the *Barn Dance* and the *Sunday Morning Gatherin'*. Vernon was one of the nicest people I think I ever met, had one of the winningest personalities of anybody that I know. Even if he couldn't have sung a lick, he could win the audience with that Rainwater smile. The only disappointment he caused was to the young girls in the audience who had to learn he was already taken.

Lair's daughters Jenny Lee and Ann Henderson began to take over more and more of the behind-the-scenes operation for their eighty-four-year-old dad. It was Ann Henderson, proprietor of the Westward Ho Square Dance Shop in Renfro Valley, who was the driving force behind a square dance festival that enjoyed instant success. It became an annual event and brought about a little Square Dance Hall of Fame in the back room of our Renfro Valley radio station. Although it didn't continue to grow much after its earlier success, it may have been more important to Renfro Valley than anyone could ever imagine. It was one of the square dance callers who brought along just for the ride, a young lady schoolteacher, Susan Tomes, who became one of our most talented entertainers.

In the month of June of that thirty-ninth season a little bit of history was made when Mr. Lair gave his audience a shortened *Barn Dance* show and turned a young country entertainer and his band loose to entertain for the major part of the time. It was this young man's first time in the Valley and so far his last. But to say that he was well-received would be an understatement. He has never had a hit record or a TV show and his name is not a household word, but when you see him perform, you don't soon forget. Clyde Foley Cummins comes by his talent naturally. His mother was *Barn Dance* entertainer Betty Foley. His father, Bentley, is an uncle of Jan Cummins, and he is first cousin to Pat Boone's daughter, Debby. Mr. Lair's invitation to Clyde and Clyde's performance were both given, it seemed, to honor Mr. Lair's long-time friend and Clyde's grandpa, the late "Ramblin" Red Foley.

Young and talented, Lou Ann Stigall joined the *Barn Dance* and *Gatherin'*, and Jo Nell Fisher was once again a featured vocalist on both shows.

July was a sad time. Mrs. Cloie Smith, the widow of Alfie Smith, owner of the Lodge and Motel and Mr. Lair's partner, died on July 25 of 1978.

Renfro Valley has had a harvest festival of sorts off and on over the years, but it wasn't until the fall of 1979 that Jenny Lee and her husband, Wayne King, were given permission to hold their own private harvest festival on Renfro Valley property. I wondered a few times why this wasn't a Renfro Valley project and if this out-of-the-company but still-in-the-family maneuver wasn't a little bit of clever planning. I don't suppose it bothered anyone. I doubt if anyone really thought that Jenny Lee and Wayne could pull this off, not the first year at least. But if that was the thinking they were wrong. This festival was a success right from the start. It was like folks were just waiting for it to happen. They called it Renfro Valley's 'Lasses Making and Country Music Gatherin'. This event, now referred to as the Harvest Festival, has been successful for the past eighteen years, and if last year is any indication, it will be around for a few years more. Richard Mullins, longtime caretaker at the Salt Peter Cave property, was the first 'lasses maker and continued for a number of years at that job.

At the close of the year, Ralph Gabbard found his way into the Valley, this time to film a pilot of the Renfro Valley *Gatherin'*. We were wondering recently if that pilot is still lying around someplace. Even though it was of little value at the time for one reason or the other, today it would definitely be a valuable addition to our archives. As far as I know it would be the only video of the *Gatherin'* with John Lair as narrator.

1980s

Memorable Days

The forty-first season of the *Renfro Valley Barn Dance* opened up in the spring of 1980, coming in like a lamb and going out the same way. When Susan Tomes joined the Renfro Valley Folks it was the biggest news event I can think of, but for some reason our little newspaper didn't even give her a mention. She didn't even make it into Virginia Sutton's new cookbook, which published favorite recipes of Virginia's and other talent on the *Barn Dance*. It could be that the book was too far along in its planning before Susan joined us or it could be that Susan doesn't know how to cook. I don't know. I just know that it wasn't until the February issue of the *Bugle* in 1981 that Susan's picture appeared with a note that she was a new member of the *Renfro Valley Barn Dance* and our 1981 Valentine.

I was the master of ceremonies on that night, and I remember introducing a pretty little black-haired girl with a last name that gave me a little trouble. It was Susan Tomes, and Susan was too good to be true. Her song, "One Day at a Time," brought the audience to their feet, and they wouldn't stop applauding until we promised to let her do another. Only problem was, she didn't know another, so she sang "One Day at a Time" through once again. The audience loved it, and so did John Lair. We came to find out, Susan knew more than one song, but she just wasn't sure of herself. Between that day and this, I wouldn't be surprised if she hasn't been on more Renfro Valley Shows than any other one entertainer.

"Country" Charlie Napier, another schoolteacher with a love for the spotlight, joined WRVK as a salesman and found his way over to the *Barn Dance* stage for a little novelty singing on a Saturday night.

He soon became emcee partner with Al Ballinger. Mr. Lair became one step closer to sole ownership of Renfro Valley when he and his partner, Gary Smith, were successful in buying out Glen Pennington. Glen's duties as emcee on the Red Barn *Jamboree* were turned over to Charlie Harrison and Linville Ball. Jim Gaskin's appearance on stage as a regular on the *Barn Dance* topped the list of happenings of importance in 1981.

Sometime during the early eighties I received a call from my friend Don Warden, who was then, as now, Dolly Parton's personal and business manager. He wanted to know if I knew of anyone in the area that still talked the way that country folks used to talk in the mountains. My thoughts went immediately to two fellers I work with on the *Barn Dance*, the Baker brothers, Bob and Jess. It wasn't that they had the mountain dialect so much as they drew out their words and put a twang to 'em like no one I knew. When I mentioned them, Don wanted to know if they would mind meeting with some folks who wanted to learn from them. I assured him that they would not mind at all.

He then told me that Jane Fonda was planning to make a movie, *The Doll Maker,* and that the movie was set in the Kentucky mountains. If everything went according to plan, Jane and Dolly would come up later that summer. He said they would call me when they were 75 or 100 miles out and that would give me time to get in touch with Bob and Jess and get them to the radio station, where we would meet. Absolute secrecy was a must. I shouldn't even tell Bob and Jess unless I absolutely had to. I wondered later just how I would approach Jess, as I didn't really know if he knew he talked any different from anyone else. When I called him I started by telling him that some important people were planning to make a movie and wanted to hear some real country talk and wondered if he could help. "Helllll, yes," he said, "I know somebody that is jest as country as anybody you'd be lookin' fer. My uncle and aint talks as country as you'd ever want."

I decided right then I didn't have to tell Jess that he was the one I had in mind. I just explained to him the circumstances as I knew them and admitted that I couldn't tell him who would be involved. He said that didn't matter. I'm sure he figured that Dolly maybe was in the background there someplace, so we didn't say.

Two or three months later I got a call from Don. He apologized for the sudden notice. Instead of 100 miles out, he was already in Renfro Valley. The three of them had driven up on Dolly's tour bus. I told them to come on up to the radio station about a mile up the road and I would call the Bakers. Jess was out in his garden when I called, and he said he was not fit to meet with folks. I told him that it just didn't matter, that we needed to move on and to get Bob and come on up. The bus rolled in and parked out in front of KOA campground next door to WRVK. Dolly, Jane, and Don came in. I showed them around the station while we waited for the Bakers. This was late in the day, and our sales staff, Charlie Napier, was in the station when they arrived. I thought for sure he was going to explode. Now, he'd met Dolly about seven or eight years before that and he hadn't got over that yet. And now here he was in the same room with Dolly Parton and Jane Fonda! Whatever he was working on as far as the station's sales were concerned went out the window for the moment.

Bob and Jess arrived, and it was decided that an extra car was needed to chauffeur the ladies around so Bob and Jess wouldn't have to drive all the way back to the station when their visit was over. Well, Charlie popped up real quick and offered to loan his car or to loan it and drive it, which they accepted. The first step was Jess's house, where he lived the life of a long-time bachelor. He had fried him some potatoes that morning or the evening before, and they were still in the skillet on the stove where Dolly, with a fork in her hand, found them. Jess talked until the day he died about Dolly Parton eating his fried taters. They went from there to the home of Bob and Jess's aunt and uncle out on a little farm in the country and, according to Don later, found just exactly what they were looking for. The fact of the matter is, it was so perfect that Jane decided that she would return and spend some time there. There was a little smokehouse out back where she had planned to live, getting a taste of the rough mountain life that she was to portray.

The excitement of the celebrities visiting the county soon wore off and speculation as to whether Jane would return took over. And that died later as time passed on. It was a year or more later when I came into the *Barn Dance* one Saturday night and found Bob and Jess fuming at the mouth. Jane had returned, just like she planned to do, and had been there a whole week before Bob and Jess found out. Jess said, "Hell fire, I was the one that introduced her to 'em in the first place and then they didn't have the courtesy to let me know she was back." Of course, Mr. and Mrs. Baker were just obeying her request that no one know she was there. She wasn't out on the farm, I might add. Between that first visit and her return the Bakers had decided that they would give up farm life. They'd sold the place and moved to an apartment in Mt. Vernon.

For most of two weeks Jane Fonda spent time with the Bakers, listening and learning and jogging on the streets of Mt. Vernon in the early morning hours without being recognized by the townfolks. Now, the next time Turner Classic Movies presents *The Doll Maker*, you'll know the part little Renfro Valley played in its making.

Jimmy Jackson joined our roster in 1981. Red and Sharon Creech were now the sweetheart duet team of the *Barn Dance*. Doc Jack Lewis brought his steel guitar back over from the Red Barn *Jamboree* and settled in on the *Barn Dance*. And the talents of both the *Barn Dance* and the *Jamboree* were invited to Knoxville to perform at the World's Fair. Once again, I didn't get to go. My involvement at the WRVK radio station kept me in the Valley.

But the fall of 1982 was anything but uneventful. First, John Lair was picked as one of the finalists to be nominated for the Country Music Hall of Fame, an honor he certainly deserved, but he lost out to someone I know was just as deserving. More unfortunately, while attending the ceremonies in Nashville, Mr. Lair suffered a stroke that took a toll on his life.

Frankie Denny and her sister, Mary Ann Martin, organized the John Lair and *Bugle* fan clubs in 1983. Mary Ann and Frankie had been dyed-in-the-wool Renfro Valley fans since first hearing a *Renfro Valley Barn Dance* broadcast. Their first visit to the Valley came in 1967, and they haven't missed an opening show to this day. Jo Nell Fisher and Kit Simunick were in Renfro Valley following their wedding at Gross Pointe, Michigan, at the close of Renfro Valley's forty-fourth season. Also about this time we were saddened by the news of the untimely death of Merle Travis, long-time friend of John Lair and the Renfro Valley Folks. Mr. Lair was not able to attend that funeral, but he was represented by Marge and Debby Rhoads, a mother and daughter team from western Kentucky who had joined the *Barn Dance* at the suggestion of their cousin, Merle. Marge and Debby were around for quite some time on the *Barn Dance* and the *Sunday Morning Gatherin'*. I was proud to have them in my all-girl band, the Girls of the Barndance. Vocalist Ray Holliday had joined the *Barn Dance* along with a couple of western Kentucky boys, Ronnie Matthews and Tim Sisko.

Mr. Lair was having trouble with his speech. Even though he was continuing with the *Gatherin'*, he would soon turn that chore over to

Jim Gaskin. Patty Towery was the new organist on the *Gatherin'* and Elmer Goodman, long-time supporter of Renfro Valley and a true, traditional country music vocalist, joined the *Barn Dance* after a life-time of waiting.

The 1984 season opened up at the *Renfro Valley Jamboree* with Debbie Shipley, a new vocalist from Frankfort, making a hit before the Renfro Valley audience. Mr. Lair was made proud when his grandson, John J. Teater, was the emcee of the annual John Lair Day Talent Contest in 1984. I believe Mr. Lair had plans to groom young John to take over responsibility for the *Renfro Valley Barn Dance.* As Mr. Lair's health continued to fail, Johnny J. was slowly improving from an automobile accident that had almost taken his life. But John's own health took a turn for the worse a few months later, forcing him to give up his new job. That accident eventually did take the life of young John.

Soon Mr. Lair was no longer able to attend the shows except on special occasions. He was present at the final show of our forty-fifth season and was present at the Christmas party that year.

Patty Flye and husband, Ralph Peavy, returned to the Valley in 1984, and, from North Carolina, Grady Hockett and Dave Osborn joined the *Barn Dance,* giving their audiences some mighty fine entertainment for a few years before they decided to return to their home state and open up their own show.

Buck McKenzie had joined the *Renfro Valley Barn Dance* along the way. Buck was a fine vocalist who had almost nearly, but not quite hardly, made it as a recording artist a couple of times before coming to the Valley.

Jess Baker of the team of Bob and Jess died in June 1985, and Bob asked Jim Gaskin to join him as a singing partner in Jess's place. Bob and Jim became close friends and remained singing partners until Bob's death a few years later.

In June 1985 Lily May of the Coon Creek Girls at sixty-eight years old was one of twelve to win a National Heritage Award from the National Endowment for the Arts. The award to Lily May, the country's highest honor for achievement in a traditional arts field, carried a $5,000 prize. She was in the hospital and considered too ill to react to the honor. She died on Sunday, July 15, in Lexington. I know this honor would have made Mr. Lair proud had he known. His own death came less than four months later at the age of ninety-one. John Lair, founder of the now world-famous Renfro Valley, just one week following his forty-sixth anniversary, moved away once more, this time for good.

We will never know all that Mr. Lair had in mind for Renfro Valley when at the age of eighty-two he started on the road to sole ownership once again. But I have an idea that he accomplished most of what he set out to do—to finish his life on stage at the Old Barn and leave the *Barn Dance* intact for his daughters.

From Out of the Wings

Only two of John Lair's four daughters, Ann Henderson and Jenny Lee King, were in a position to lend a hand in the operation. Nancy and Barbara lived too far away to be of much help. Jenny Lee was the first to step out of the wings. She began helping Mr. Lair prior to his death with the *Bugle* and promoting the Valley at various tourist functions around the state. She was also promoting some special events, especially her 'Lasses Festival each October.

After a while Ann began to take charge, and, at Mr. Lair's death, she was in the spotlight heading up the entire operation. I personally don't believe you could have found a better manager under the circumstances than Ann Henderson. She'd had no show business experience of her own and was not financially able to back any long-range goals, but she did have enough of the John Lair "feel" for the *Barn Dance* that she was able to carry it on with the same dignity that it had enjoyed for most of its forty-five years.

"Ragged but right" might have been a good description of our show. Ragged musically speaking, but right when it came to entertainment. Susan Tomes used to complain that everyone who owned or could borrow a guitar was out on stage at the same time, and you can bet not everyone was in time. Some of the musicians we had were as good as they come: Susan, Jim Gaskin, Patty Flye, just to name three. They top the list, I suppose. Susan, Patty, Virginia Sutton, Marge, and Debby Rhoads made up the female portion of the show.

It was this combination whom I picked to help me in my rendition of some comedy parodies. We billed ourselves as Pete Stamper and the Girls of the Barndance. And, in addition to the *Barn Dance*,

A little mistletoe goes a long way. Pete Stamper and the
Girls of the Barndance: Patty Flye, Marge Rhoads, Debby
Rhoads, Pete, Virginia Sutton, Susan Tomes.

we did a few bookings close by. This was about the time that Porter
Wagoner was sporting his all-girl band. We played off his fame for a
little fun. I used to tell the audience how much fun it was traveling
with the girls and just how economical it was. "For instance, we would
check into motels that allowed you to cook in the room because all of
them cooked and we could save on food like that (and we never had to
rent but two rooms). We shouldn't have had to have rented but one;
however, Susan Tomes demanded that she have a room to herself."

The best music was probably being performed on stage at the
Red Barn for at least a part of this time. I say probably, because like
most of the *Barn Dance* entertainers, the *Jamboree* cast across the
road came in from around the country for their show. Our shows were
scheduled at the same time, so I never made it over there on their side
of the road on Saturday nights. But today I am doing my comedy act,
sometimes emceeing the *Jamboree* and am well acquainted with some
of that same old talent, knowing what they can do. Coming to us from
across the Tennessee line from around the Cumberland Gap area were

Don Gulley, Steve Gulley, Mark Laws, and Jerry Evans. Now, when you put these four fellows together, you've got some good music. But there was some little problem they couldn't work out with Ann, so they went back across the border for a couple of years. We were mighty glad when Mark, Don, and Steve came back around 1990. Since that time they have put down roots in both our *Barn Dance* and our *Jamboree,* and they are a viable part of every piece of music we play.

Others who found their way to the *Jamboree* were Donny Chastene, Roger Drake, Ernie Sowder, Steve Sears, Roger McClure, Mark Christopher, Steve Hays, Ray Harrison, Bill Lovern, Ray Brandenburg, Sonny Morgan, Charlie Harrison, and Chris Robbins. The ladies at the Red Barn included Sue Brock, Robyn and Sandy Smith, Sandy Rudder, Betty Jean Hurt, Georgianna Casey, and Debbie Shipley. It was Georgianna who said "I do" to her fiancé, Gary Goode, on stage at the Red Barn. If there were other weddings performed in front of the *Jamboree* audience in the Red Barn, I'm not aware of them.

As I may have mentioned before, the *Jamboree* had a rough row to hoe for a lot of years. When it was in competition with the *Barn Dance,* they were treated like the enemy. And after they were brought under the same umbrella as the *Barn Dance,* they were treated more like a red-headed stepchild. Tickets to the *Jamboree* and the *Barn Dance* were sold on the same location on the *Barn Dance* side of the road. And when a guest asked for a ticket, they were asked, "Old Barn, New Barn, or both." And, of course, many times this brought on the next question, "What's the difference?" And the ticket seller would say, "Well the Old Barn has the older music, the New Barn (referring to the Red Barn) has the newer music." Of course, this simplistic description of the difference was unfair to the *Jamboree.* I know a lot of tickets to the *Jamboree* went unsold because "new music" meant one thing to one person, something else to another. Mostly new music of the time we're speaking meant loud rock, and that's not what our guests came to Renfro Valley to hear—or what was played.

They were not told that in addition to a few of the more modern songs they would also hear Bluegrass, gospel, traditional country, and comedy at the Red Barn *Jamboree.* Of course, the entertainers from both the *Barn Dance* and the *Jamboree* were good friends, even kinfolk in some cases. When the shows were over, it was probable they would meet for coffee and a late supper. Not long ago Don Gulley was talking about the fact that he had never seen stage equipment in such bad shape as it was at the Red Barn. The mike stands were loose, the

Barn Dance cast of 1987. Seated: Old Joe Clark, Virginia Sutton, Vester Parker, Rhoads, Patty Flye. Standing: Pete Stamper, Bob Baker, Jim Gaskin, Grady Ballinger.

cords were knotted and frayed. I pretended to Don that it was news to me but the truth is I remember a lot of times over at the *Barn Dance* when some of our equipment began to go bad we would slip across the road and make a quick exchange.

Entertainers came and went at the *Barn Dance*, but the ones that made up pretty much the foundation of the show through a good part of the eighties were emcee and vocalist, Al Ballinger; Red and Sharon Creech; Jim and Ruby Ann Gaskin; the Rhoadses, Marge and Debby; Patty Flye; Old Joe Clark and Terry; Curt Caldwell; Bee Lucas; "Country" Charlie Napier; Bob Baker; Grady Hockett; Vester Parker; Virginia Sutton; Susan Tomes; Coy Priddy; Jo Nell Fisher; and Jan Cummins. Our music was greatly improved when Ann hired Vester Parker's young son, Jeff. Jeff Parker came to the *Barn Dance* and the *Gatherin'*, bringing his mandolin along. Jeff was an all-around musician, and he stood out, or should I say blended in, as a number one harmony singer as well. He was a valuable addition to our Renfro Valley entertainment.

Jo Nell Fisher, Coy Priddy, Susan Tomes, Terry Clark, Marge Rhoads, Debby Hockett, Curt Caldwell, Red and Sharon Creech, Ruby Ann Gaskin, and Al

Early in 1985 I had made up my mind that I would once again try to revive my career outside of Renfro Valley. I knew I had to have a record or a TV show or something to help me along. With my luck, I thought I would try for all of it. When Hal Smith, who continued to own the radio station, learned that I was thinking about leaving WRVK, he made a deal with me to help if I would stay around and help him sell the station. He and a friend would help me market a new album and, since his friend, Hays Jones, had an "in" with *Hee-Haw*'s Sam Lavello, I was told a spot on the *Hee-Haw* show was a good possibility. There were a number of local folks who were interested in WRVK radio station, but the asking price of $200,000 was keeping them away. Virginia Sutton had put together a group that was interested. Sam Ford of Ford Realty and Auction Company had an interest. Sam was only interested, he told me, if I promised to stay on, and I probably would have under his ownership, but again the price was in the way. Sam has always had an interest in Renfro Valley and its entertainers.

In front of legislature.

He once expressed to me a desire to own the place. He said it was the only thing that could take him away from his real estate career.

I spent the year recording each Saturday night, hoping to put together that routine for a new album. Mae Axton, a friend of a friend and a publicist in Nashville, helped me design a cover for my publicity material. Dolly Parton wrote a personal letter to Mr. Sam Lavello recommending me as a good addition to his show. This letter was to be delivered by Mr. Jones. I wasn't sure how long it would take to sell the station, but I was willing to wait it out. The station sold about a year later to an individual whose business practices were what I could call a little bit left of normal. I handed over my management duties and went back to work as a disc jockey.

On one of my trips to Nashville, Hays Jones told me that he hadn't had any luck. He said he probably should have delivered Dolly's letter to Sam Lavello in person, indicating that it had been mailed. For some reason, I had a feeling it had not. When I got home I wrote Jones a letter and simply asked him to return her letter to me, which he did, with a note saying, "I'm Sorry."

A portion of the comedy material I recorded on stage at the Old Barn in 1985 finally made it, becoming a part of my album *My Wife's Driving Lessons (And Other Road Side Stories)*, released just four years ago.

I had decided that I could no longer work at WRVK. I turned in my notice to Karen Noe, the secretary, and with her help I was able to leave the station with all my back pay plus two weeks' vacation pay. I was not going on vacation, however; I was booked those two weeks in Dollywood. My agreement with the folks at Dollywood was that I would be there two weeks and three Saturdays; however, on a special arrangement I could come back home for the second Saturday and work a show that had been booked for some time. It was billed as the First Annual Red Foley Homecoming and was promoted by WRVK. I was scheduled to make an appearance with my Girls of the Barndance and also to emcee part of the show. The headliner was to be Pat Boone, along with about fifteen past and present stars of the Grand Ole Opry, such as Lonzo and Oscar, Jimmy Dickens, Melba Montgomery, the Nashville Brass, Redd Stewart, and a number of others. Pat was paid in advance and made his appearance. But many of the others wouldn't take the gamble and stayed home. So did the crowd. The only lasting result of this event was the naming of a road in honor of Red Foley.

Ann Henderson approached me about coming to work for her in 1987. It was on this weekend that I finalized my deal with Ann and came to work as her assistant in helping direct the entertainment at the *Renfro Valley Barn Dance*. One of the first things we did together was working on a reunion day celebration. It was scheduled for September 5, 1987, and turned out to be one of the best reunions you could have ever asked for. This was an annual event, but we were never able to top it. A good many of the early entertainers had made their homes in far away places and were unable to attend each year and those of later vintage either hadn't been away long enough or lived too close by to really be interested in a get-together. A reunion of pioneers of country music sponsored by CMA and Grand Ole Opry was very successful for a few short years but was soon dropped. I always enjoyed our reunions and was sorry to see them discontinued. They were so much fun, and I always learned a little bit more about Renfro Valley each time we'd get together.

At one reunion I was reminded of the liveliest show the *Barn Dance* had ever seen. It took place in about 1973 or 1974, according to Bob England, the *Barn Dance* steel player at the time. According to Bob it was a Saturday night like any other at 7:30 P.M. when the show got under way before a packed house. Bob was at his steel guitar for the first few minutes of the show. Then he got a break and took a seat on the bales of hay that served as seating on the stage of the Old Barn at that time. In just a few short minutes, Bob felt a burning and itching on the end of his backbone. To tell it like it was, his butt was on fire. Now, this was happening to about a half-dozen of the other entertainers, but no one would mention it. The problem was, how do you rub or scratch in a place like that in front of hundreds of people? That is, anyone but Bun Wilson. Well, if you had been there that night, you would know. You do such things as clog, squirm, prance, sit down, stand up, anything that keeps you moving. Everybody thought their affliction was personal until after the show when one poor soul couldn't stand it any longer and mentioned that he was "itchin' in his britchen." That's when the truth came out. It was learned that everyone who had sat for any time on the bales of hay had this same discomfort. It was learned later that the hay had been sprayed during the week with some kind of fire retardant and that's why everyone had "ants in their pants."

On February 9, 1988, I was part of a troupe of *Barn Dance* performers who made an appearance during a session of the Kentucky House of Representatives. We—Virginia Sutton, Patty Flye, Bee Lucas, Susan Tomes and Jan Cummings and I—were there at the request of Danny Ford, our representative, who offered a bill that would designate Renfro Valley as the location for the Kentucky Country Music Hall of Fame. The votes were unanimous, and the bill passed. Ten years later we are still waiting for a Hall of Fame. And, in fact, Governor Patton has set aside over $2 million to build the museum, which will occupy part of John Lair's old home place. I still have hopes that it will happen one of these days. With our history and now the prospect of a bright future, I can think of no place in the state where a country music museum and Hall of Fame would be enjoyed by more people than at Renfro Valley.

As the new season got under way in the spring of 1988, Ann mentioned she would like to have one more special event and asked if I had any ideas. I had one that I had held onto for more than twenty years. Bun Wilson and I had dreamed and planned an all-comedy show back when he was making guest appearances on the *Barn Dance* during the two years that Hal Smith, Hank Cochran, Ray Price, and Willie Nelson had the place leased. I hadn't seen much of Bun in twenty years, but I had an idea that he would be all for trying it out. The event was to be called the Renfro Valley Comedy Daze. Ann listened to my description of what I had planned and gave me the go-ahead. I

Comedy Daze 1988. Front: Pete Stamper, Eric Eversole, Susan Tomes, Wilful Stumble, Jennifer Coffey, Bun Wilson, Ethan Eversole, Jan Cummins. Standing: Emory Martin, Lonzo and Oscar, Cousin Leo, Linda Lou Martin, Patty Flye, Virginia Sutton, Old Joe Clark, Jim and Ruby Ann Gaskin, Speck Rhodes, Eugene Brown.

made contact with some old friends who I thought would do me a favor and work for a little less than usual, and we set a date for July 22 and 23. There were Lonzo and Oscar, thirty-year veterans of the Grand Ole Opry; Speck Rhodes, comedy star of the long-running *Porter Wagoner Show;* James "Goober" Buchanan, the south's craziest nut; a character who billed himself as Willful Stumble and His Watzit; and Eugene Brown impersonating Grandpa Jones. Judge Ray Korns took time out from the bench to lend a hand. From the *Barn Dance,* Old Joe Clark; Jerry Issacs, the Chicken Man; Jim Gaskin and the Girls of the Barndance also had a part. Those of us from Renfro Valley had a few skits and comedy songs that we had run through a time or two, and we wove them in and around our guest comedians.

For a show with no dress rehearsal and not even a complete run-through, it came off well. We had folk who bought tickets to both nights and promised they'd be back the following year. I wasn't sure that there would be a next year, because I had heard a rumor from a pretty good source that Glen Pennington and Ralph Gabbard were trying to buy Renfro Valley. As the rumors grew stronger and the denials grew weaker, late in the year Ann invited me to attend a meeting of the Fifth District tourist interest held in Cumberland Falls. The meeting was headed up by Fifth District congressman Harold Rogers, a long-time friend of Renfro Valley. The guest speaker was Jack Hirschend, one of two brothers who owned Silver Dollar City in Branson, Missouri, and Dollywood in Tennessee. On the way down Ann said she thought she owed it to me to give me the facts in the matter of a sale since I might want to make some plans accordingly. She told me that she was almost sure she would sell the Valley. She said she didn't want to, but that she realized there was no possible way that she could operate it the way that she knew it should be operated. She did say that she hoped to delay the sale for a year. She wanted to keep the Valley in the family in its fiftieth year.

I'll never forget that meeting. I sat at one end of the table with Ann. Glen Pennington and Ralph Gabbard sat across from us at another table. As Mr. Hirschend talked about all the things that could be possible for the future of the Fifth District and what an important role Renfro Valley would play in it all, I sat there feeling proud to have been a part of Renfro Valley's past. And, as I looked across the room at Glen and Ralph, I wondered if there would be a place for a worn-out comic in its future.

On the way back home Ann and I continued to talk about the future of the Valley and the part that it might play in the hopes and dreams that we'd heard discussed at the Fifth District congressional meeting. I found myself weighing every possibility carefully, as I knew that whatever happened was going to affect my life in a big way. I personally liked Ann and enjoyed working for her. As a matter of fact, she was paying me more money for my work than I had ever made in the Valley before. Because I could see so much of her daddy in her, I knew how much it would mean for her to be able to keep the Valley in its fiftieth year. At the same time, like her, I felt the Valley's future would be brighter if it was bought by the right people. I had all the confidence in the world in Glen Pennington and Ralph Gabbard. I had had enough experience in life's deals, big and small, to know that a year is a long time for something to stay the same, even in the "valley where time stands still." And for that reason my better judgment told me to hope for a quick sale, even though it might mean that I would have to leave the Valley once again.

Exciting Times and Exciting People

In the next few days, remembering I once loaned a spare and waited and got left behind, I decided I could not afford to wait this time. So, after talking it over with Minnie Lee, I decided I would go looking for a job in Branson, Missouri. She liked the years that we'd lived in Springfield and thought she would like to live there again. A friend of mine at Dollywood gave me the name of the lady who booked the talent for Silver Dollar City and some of the other shows, so I gave her a call. This was early in January 1989. She told me she did not know of an opening in Branson, but she did have a job down in Arkansas that I might be interested in. I told her I would prefer Branson, but I would let her know. She then told me about a steakhouse there in Branson that showcased talent during the winter months on Monday night of each week. She told me that many of the owners of the various shows attended these performances and suggested that I might give that a try. I called the number she gave me as soon as our conversation was over and set up a spot on the show for the following Monday night.

I made another call to my buddy, Bun Wilson in Clarksville, Tennessee, and told him my plans and invited him to make the trip with me. I don't suppose we'd had a chance to visit more than a half a dozen times in the twenty-two years following his appearances on the *Renfro Valley Barn Dance*. This would give us plenty of time to reminisce and laugh the way we always managed to do when we were together. It gave us more time than I really expected, for I made the mistake of letting Bun read the map and he found us a shortcut— maybe as the crow flies. For hours it seemed we went up and down and around and over and under those Ozark hills. I thought we were never going to get out of the woods. At one point I told Bun to turn the heater down, that I was getting a little hot. He told me the heater was already down, that I was just going through the change of life. I said, "Well, good. It's the only thing I've been through in the past hundred miles." It wasn't a great ad lib line, but it still tickles Bun even today.

At the show the following night it could not have gone any better for me. The place was packed and, even though I did not know it at the time, I was competing with other talent. In fact, I beat out eight other performers. When I finished my routine, I left the stage and walked back over to the table to watch the rest of the show. I was greeted there by a man who complimented me on my performance, told me that he was one of the owners of the *Baldknobbers* show, an old, established show in that area, and he wanted to know if I was interested in a job. He said he appreciated my clean comedy, and, as they had a family-type show, he thought I would fit right in. He went on to say that he would pay me $600 per week, fifty-two weeks out of the year, hospitalization and $25,000 life insurance, and when the season closed in Branson, I would be traveling with the show around the western states on personal appearances. We shook hands with the understanding that I would give him a definite yes or no in a few days. That's when I learned that this was a competition. He was one of the judges and, to my surprise, when the show was over, my name was called; I went back to the stage to receive my first prize: my little trophy—"It's Show Biz"—and $75. I still have the trophy . . . and the $75 we spent on the way home.

I picked the route home that took us by quite a few little food joints. On the way back I told Bun that I was going to call the man and take the deal. I had told Bun about the changes that might take place in Renfro Valley and suggested to him that it might be something that he would be interested in a little later. He said he doubted it. With his camper sales business in Clarksville, Tennessee, he wouldn't want to move away. He said it was too far to drive each week.

I arrived back in Renfro Valley Tuesday night, and Wednesday morning I put my call in to Mr. Baldknobber as he had asked me to do. He was out on my first call; I left my number. I just missed him on my second call; I reminded them that they had my number. He had gone for the day on my third call. After just missing him the next day I did manage to talk to a musician friend I had worked with in Springfield, Missouri, a few years earlier who was a member of his show. I don't know if he did not have the details or maybe just hated to tell me, but I finally concluded that cold water had been thrown on Mr. Baldknobber's decision to hire me, possibly by a brother and partner in the business. As my little trophy reminded me, "It's Show Biz." Well, I would just go back the following Monday, as they had invited me to do, and try again.

On the Saturday before I was to leave, Glen Pennington came to the Valley and asked me ride up to Druther's Restaurant for a cup of coffee. At Druther's he said that he was going to break a rule and confide in me some confidential information about plans for buying Renfro Valley. He told me that he was breaking this rule because he had heard that I was planning to leave and he would like to convince me to stay. He told me the sale would be right away and that they would not wait a year, that they had secretly purchased that piece of land on the south side of Renfro Creek that John Lair had recently bought and lost for nonpayment. And if by some chance they could not reach an agreement for the *Barn Dance,* they were prepared to build a new barn and a new show. In any case, he wanted me to stay. He asked me what I was doing for Ann in addition to my *Barn Dance* performance and work on the *Gatherin',* with which he was acquainted, and wanted to know how much I was making. When I told him, he assured me that I would make as much. He said that he would be the entertainment director and that he wanted me to assume the role of his assistant.

He then informed me that he was in the audience in July 1988 at our Comedy Daze special, and he asked me if I could put a show together similar to that but on a weekly basis. He said he wanted to make the *Jamboree* as different from the *Barn Dance* as possible and yet he wanted it to remain traditional country music and he thought a comedy show might be what he was looking for. I told him I could do it if I could manage to hire one of two comedians, either Bun Wilson or James "Goober" Buchanan. I knew that it would take the old country vaudeville skits to carry this kind of a show, and they were the only ones I knew who knew a number of these routines and how they were done. Glen said something then that I will never forget because it told me that things were about to change in Renfro Valley. He said, "Why not get both of them?" Getting two of something when you might get by with just one was not the normal way of operating at Renfro Valley. I went away from Druthers with my druthers that day. I was so glad Mr. Baldknobber had changed his mind, for whatever reason. If he had hired me I probably would have followed through in spite of the fact that I preferred to stay in Renfro Valley.

Renfro Valley's fiftieth season could not have gotten under way any better than it did. The transfer from one to the other came off perfectly, it seemed to me. It was the old and the new walking side by side. The brochures for that season were prepared in the fall of 1988, so they had the John Lair flavor. The new owners put together a fiftieth anniversary keepsake album that was first class in every respect. Most of the talent from the *Barn Dance* stayed on with the new owners and were joined by some of the best talent the Renfro Valley stage had ever held. Glen Pennington did himself and the Valley proud with the choices he made. Not only were these fine musicians and vocalists but, just as important, if not more so, they were fine people morally and in every other way. Most of the talent that joined the *Barn Dance* and the *Jamboree* in 1989, are still with us today.

My part in the talent lineup, as I mentioned, was to hire Bun Wilson and James "Goober" Buchanan. When the season opened in March, I had failed in both cases. "Goober" was then eighty-one years young and thought the drive up from Nashville each week would just be more than he wanted to tackle. The best he could promise would be a guest appearance on the show from time to time. This was something that we would be looking forward to, but I needed someone there who was going to walk on that stage every Saturday night. The most I could get out of Bun Wilson was that he would promise me he would give it a try for two or three weeks and check it out. I don't believe the third week had gone by before Bun was in Ralph Gabbard's office signing that fifty-two-week contract. Now, I wasn't the one to reward him financially, but I can take credit for helping put together a show that played to Bun's biggest weakness—a format that let him be funnier longer than he had ever been before. There would be no more "Hold it to two minutes, Bun" for the next four years.

I can't overestimate the value of Glen's talent scouting for his new Renfro Valley shows. He had been planning this venture for a long time, and it paid off. He made few mistakes in the additions that he brought to the *Barn Dance* and the *Jamboree*. Oh, there were two or three who didn't work out for one reason or other, one or two who didn't fit in really with our Renfro Valley family. A good part of them had been tried and tested, as they had worked for his *Jamboree* show in earlier years.

Clyde Foley, a musician's musician.

Glen let me feel like the *Jamboree* was my show by first conferring with me before he brought on a new act. There was one exception that I remember. He came to me one day in the studio where I was working and told me that he had hired me a guitar man. He was aware that I knew of him, even though he wasn't sure I knew him. I only knew of Clyde Foley, even though I knew his mother quite well and was fairly well acquainted with his father. If there ever was an artist who had a right to the Renfro Valley stage, it was Clyde Foley. His mother was Rosey of the original Coon Creek Girls, his father was Cotton Foley, one of the Renfro Valley founders, and his uncle was Red Foley. Clyde was an exceptional musician, but Glen felt that he

First cast picture of the new administration in 1989. Front: Bill Kramer, Bobby Susan Tomes, Virginia Sutton, Pete Stamper, Carrie Stone, Old Joe Clark, Dale Cummins, Ronnie Parker, Vester Parker, Donna Faye, Jerry Isaacs, Donna Dailey, Thompson, Terry Clark, Billy Wagers, Renee Marshall, David Marshall. Back

owed me a warning about him. Clyde was an introvert. He kept to himself, and he kept his feelings to himself, and it had been his habit over the years when he became dissatisfied, disgruntled over something, he would not try to work things out or even let it be known, he would just walk away with no notice or good-byes. Glen told me that he was fairly sure Clyde would be on our show that following Saturday night, but from there on out it was anybody's guess. But he did assure me that when Clyde was there, there would be a lot of guitar pickin' going on. He said he might stay a month, he might even stay six months, but if he stayed a year that would be longer than he ever stayed anyplace else.

Pennington, Amy Carlin, Glen Pennington, Vivian Pennington, Ernie Sowder,
Ann Bradley, Jeff Watson. Second row: Don Gulley, David Osborn, Jan
Bun Wilson, Jim Gaskin, Chubby Howard, Bobby Sloan, Clyde Foley, Glenn
row: Steve Gulley, Eric Eversole, Ethan Eversole, Shane Thompson, Jeff Parker.

I found Clyde to be easygoing. He had a dry but terrific sense of
humor, and we hit it off from the start. For a little while he helped me
in the studio with the production of the *Sunday Morning Gatherin'*,
and we became well acquainted. Clyde loved performing on the
Gatherin', as the old songs gave him a challenge to his musical talents. It wasn't long until the possibility of Clyde leaving was the fur-
thest from my mind. And then, after about three years, Clyde came to
me one day and told me that he was considering leaving. Actually his
mind was already made up. He was forced to leave before the end of
our season in order to be assured of a wintertime job; the difference
from his past was that he was coming by to say good-bye. I told him

that we would like for him to think it over a little longer and that if he did leave, I was sure that he would be welcomed back anytime. We hated to see Clyde leave.

We did not hire a new replacement for the *Jamboree*. Glenn Thompson came over from the *Barn Dance* and filled that spot. We finished up the season with Glenn working both shows. During the winter months, a short time before our next season was to open, word came to me that Clyde would like to come back, and I'll never forget the day I called. He answered the phone and I told him who I was, and then there was a long, long silence. The next voice I heard was that of his wife, Barbara. She told me that Clyde couldn't talk to me right then and asked if I would please call back in an hour. When I called back she answered the phone and told me that Clyde was outside, that she would call him in. Then she told me what had happened earlier. Clyde wanted to come back to the Valley so bad that when I first called, he was so sure I was calling to tell him that the job was no longer there for him that he just simply fell apart. I believe having the opportunity to invite Clyde Foley back to the show was the most rewarding moment of my three years as Renfro Valley's entertainment director. About mid-season, although he didn't talk about it, we became aware that Clyde was ill. It was all he could do to carry his guitar from one barn to the other. This quiet, private, gentle soul soon had to leave our stage forever, as cancer of the lung was taking its toll. Before Clyde's untimely death, I had the opportunity of recording a novelty number with Clyde, and I included it on my comedy tape, *My Wife's Driving Lessons*. Part of the liner notes on that tape read, "Clyde, I know your Uncle Red would be proud. I would like to add here that all of us at Renfro Valley were proud of our friend, Clyde Foley."

1989 News from the Bugle

January and February 1989 were business as usual. The January story in the *Bugle* announcing the special events for the year that had been set on our calendar the previous fall caused us to look back over the first fifty years in the life and times of our little valley. We had decided on a special gospel sing for April and the second annual Family Night, also in April. This event recognized the families of our guests and entertainers alike, since family has always been important at Renfro Valley. Susan Tomes received special recognition for having the most family members in the audience that night. Other events that year included the Square Dance Weekend, the Dogwood Craft Fair, Antique Car Show, Mountain Music Celebration, the John Lair Day Talent Contest, Country Comedy Daze, the annual *All-Night Sing,* Reunion Day, Molasses Festival, and the Fiddlers' Convention.

The February issue of the *Bugle* tooted its own horn in recognizing its forty-fifth birthday. It also printed the picture of the newest act on the *Renfro Valley Barn Dance,* Eric and Ethan, the Eversole Brothers. I had met these two youngsters a few months earlier when I was invited to take my guitar and entertain at the Roundstone School, where their mother taught my young grandson, John. Eric and Ethan performed on that show that afternoon, and I was quick to recognize that they were a most unusual act. They were so young, yet their music was as authentic mountain music as it could be. There are a few acts that have come along in recent years that make me wish John Lair could have been around to enjoy them, and the Eversole Brothers are one of these acts. After our meeting I invited them to appear on our

Comedy Daze Special Event, and they were hired a short time later as regular Renfro Valley Folks.

The March issue of the *Bugle* continued to look back over Renfro Valley's fifty-year history spotlighting the forty-nine years of the Renfro Valley U.S. Post Office and noting that it first opened for business in a little corner of the Renfro Valley Lodge in 1940. And the first postmaster was Virginia Crawford Lair, Mrs. John Lair. Since that time the post office has been located in the back room of the country store, now our music store; in a room that was added to the back of the museum building; in a special addition to the side of the little candy kitchen; and finally it moved to its present location in its own building on Main Street of Renfro Village. In its almost sixty years of service, there have only been four postmasters and, with one exception, they all are from the same family. After Mrs. Lair, there was Dorothy Mullins Kelsey, John Lair's niece. Then an outsider, Betty VanWinkle, came across the hill from over in the Climax settlement to run the post office from 1977 to 1983. After that, Norma Coffey Mullins, wife of Mr. Lair's nephew Harry (better known as Little Clifford) took over as postmaster, where now more than two hundred people daily get their mail. Norma is a native of Renfro Valley and once worked with the original Coon Creek Girls.

Word came from the Lair family in the March issue, and it was the most important news of the month. It was announced that the Lairs were stepping aside from the "valley where time stood still." In my mind the good-bye seemed to indicate everything fine and good about the Valley might be coming to an end. This was not the feeling of the majority of the entertainers. I think a few of us old-timers recognized the fact that John Lair's Renfro Valley had ceased to exist a long time ago and that for at least the last thirty years we had only been living in the shadows of what once had been. Even in the shadows we had held on to those things fine and good, and we had no doubt that we could take them with us on into the future.

I noted in my April article for the *Bugle* that Chris Robbins, Sandy Rudder, and Betty Jean Hurt, entertainers from the previous year, would continue with the *Jamboree*. And we added Brother, a comedy act that had worked the show in its early years. From the *Barn Dance*, Jim and his wife, Ruby Ann, joined the show, but put aside their sweetheart duets for a cornball novelty act they had performed for our comedy days special the year before, Jim portraying the comedy fiddler, Slim Miller. Young Shelly Rand, who had only appeared with us as a guest the year before, came on as a regular along with a new sister act, Kathy, Gleanna, and Cindy, the Chaney Sisters.

Celeste Prewitt, vocalist from nearby Garrard County, joined the *Jamboree.* She was a sister of a young singer I had worked with for a while on the *Barn Dance* in the late seventies whose stage name was Melissa Dean. Melissa had a fine voice and a great stage personality. Hardly a Saturday night's performance went by that she didn't get an encore from the *Barn Dance* audience. I don't recall the name of the song that helped Melissa win that applause, I can just remember it as an up-tempo little ditty. For some reason, John either didn't like the song or didn't like the reaction it was getting with the audience, I never knew which, but I do remember the night that he told Melissa she could not do that song any longer. This was very confusing to Melissa, who thought she was doing everything right. She came to me for a reason why, and I didn't have one.

I was the master of ceremonies of the portion of the show she was working, so she talked to me about her feelings on a number of occasions. One night she called me off to the side to tell me that she was leaving and that this would be her last performance. On this Saturday night she was scheduled to go on twice. Once she would be introduced by Mr. Lair, then she would make another appearance on my portion of the show. She wanted the audience to know that she was moving on to greener pastures and asked me to include the news in my introduction. She had been offered a part in the hit recording act, Dave and Sugar, stars of the Grand Ole Opry. I've always believed that Mr. Lair saw in Melissa a star in the making and viewed her as a threat to himself and the theme of the Valley.

By the fall of 1989 the schedule of shows was expanded to a Friday night *Barn Dance,* followed by a Saturday afternoon matinee; two performances of the Saturday night *Barn Dance* from the Old Barn stage at 7:30 and 9:30 and with the *Jamboree* show at 7:30 and 9:30 in the new Red Barn; the *Sunday Morning Gatherin'* in its usual time and place, 8:30 A.M. in the Old Barn on Sunday morning; and a Sunday afternoon Good Time Festival held out on the banks of Renfro Creek featuring mostly local Bluegrass bands. This was a most ambitious schedule for Renfro Valley, but it worked. The only casualty of this lineup was the Sunday afternoon Good Time Festival. The Saturday afternoon matinee became the *Mountain Gospel Jubilee.*

This lineup took us on into the following year when the Tuesday, Wednesday and Thursday shows were added. The Tuesday shows didn't work out, but a Friday night *Jamboree* was soon added to the schedule. Now, after eight years, this schedule is still working for Renfro Valley. In fact, we've added Saturday afternoon mini-shows, three thirty-five-minute shows of traditional country, Bluegrass and comedy. Before our Saturday afternoon mini-shows began four years ago, Kentucky native and nationally known actor Gene McFall for two years performed his excellent portrayal of the legendary Will Rogers in his one-man show.

1990s

Time Stopped Standing Still

The changes in Renfro Valley were introduced by the owners to the world by visible actions. I suppose other folks in other places may have been used to things getting done on a big scale, but here in Renfro Valley we were accustomed to talking about it for at least a year before getting started. The summer of 1989 was something to write home about. It looked like Home on the Range where the bulldozers roam.

Ambitious undertakings, but Glen Pennington assured me that this group that he had hand-picked for the job were well-qualified to get it done. At the top would be Ralph Gabbard, a native of Madison County, vice-president, and general manager of WKYT-TV, a CBS af-filiated television station in Lexington. Ralph would serve as president and would oversee the marketing of the shows. Glen would be the vice-president of the corporation and would serve as its entertain-ment director. Chester Elkin, a local developer, also from nearby Berea, would supervise all the new construction, and Johnny Molen, a suc-cessful Danville accountant, would act as its secretary-treasurer. These were the new owners of Renfro Valley.

The original plans called for the completion of a new 1,500-seat air-conditioned auditorium; a new campground and motel; a trade fair and farmers market; and a pool for the motel and campground guests. The Old Barn was to be air-conditioned and used for all per-formances until the new auditorium was completed. Then it was to be converted into a museum to display the country music memora-bilia collection of Glen's long-time friend, Buddy Settles, a native of nearby Berea.

The new auditorium was to be built just to the right of the museum building in the area known as the festival grounds, which was near the creek and would face U.S. 25. The campground would run from Hummel Road, beginning where Old Joe's Restaurant now stands and extending down toward the creek past the area where the new auditorium is now located. The pool and pool house were to be built at the old motel, which was to the left of the Lodge. The new motel would go in on the grassy area in front of the log cabins, and the craft village was to be built in the area across the creek from the proposed new barn. The trade fair and farmers market was built on the far side of the festival grounds at the foot of the hill behind the truck stop.

I heard more about the trade fair and farmers market, which opened in the summer of 1989, than I did about anything else for a while. It was to bring thousands and thousands into the area, I was told. However, it needed the most explaining, as folks were beginning to refer to it as Renfro Valley's flea market. It did seem to be a good idea, and I know they had high hopes for its success. It was to be patterned after one down South someone had visited recently. I don't know how much money went into the building of this fiasco, but it had to have been a tidy sum in labor costs alone. A number of first-class restrooms were built just down the hill from two lines of craft stalls that were almost unusable from the beginning. Most sat on the side of the hill, and the crafters could not set level tables to display their wares. When it rained, the combination of the stall roofs and the hillside created a flood that ran down the pathways and through many of the stalls. And the pathways were not wide enough to accommodate two cars at the same time. When one person was loading or unloading in one area, all others had to wait or risk being trapped inside. After a couple of months, it was given up as a lost cause and the buildings were dismantled. No one seemed to know who designed the layout for the trade fair. Blame was passed around. But the trade fair mistakes did not stand alone.

The campground was one long double row of pads for sixty sites, with electricity, water, and sewer that was connected to a septic tank. All lines were laid and covered and the final touches were under way when, I was told, they had to dig them up, because they had not had them inspected by the state agency that oversees such things. Now, I can't say for sure if this is correct, but I do know that they were taken up and never completed. Somewhere about this time the plans for the new auditorium were changed and later relocated on top of the abandoned campground site.

The pool house, which was later converted to the Mt. Vernon-Rockcastle County Tourism building, was started and, even though it was fairly small, it seemed to be under construction longer than any other building in the Valley. The pool was constructed on the site of a dismantled pool built by the Smith family when they owned the motel. The new pool, along with a child's wading pool, was beautiful. The large pool was decorated on the bottom with a giant painting of a guitar. I remember a great deal of concern was expressed as how to best police the crowd that the pool would attract, whether to make it available for campground and motel guests only or to open it to the public. If a decision was ever reached one way or the other, I never knew about it. Soon after the pool was filled with water it ruptured, and finally it was covered over with sand and gravel.

A decision to delay building a new motel was made, maybe because so much operating capital had gone down the drain. It might have been on the advice of Renfro Valley's first general manager, Greg Davis, who had had some experience in the hotel-motel and restaurant business. Davis came to Renfro Valley from Somerset, where he was executive director of the Southern Kentucky Tourism Development Association, responsible for helping develop tourism in the twenty-seven–county Fifth Congressional District of Kentucky. It was his efforts that had set up the meeting the previous fall that Glen, Ralph and I attended at Cumberland Falls. It was at this meeting, according to Pennington, that Ralph Gabbard decided they needed the talents of Davis. As general manager, Greg was in charge of the day-to-day operation of the company, including the restaurant and motel.

Herb and Marcheta Sparrow of Sparrow Communications, Inc., were hired to handle all of the promotions and marketing of Renfro Valley along with the special events and festivals. Herb would also edit the *Bugle*. I'll never forget a little incident that happened soon after Herb Sparrow became our *Bugle* editor. It was on Saturday night, a few minutes before showtime. Herb needed something from the recording studio, but it was locked and an alarm that was installed the day before had been set. Herb did not have access to the code, so I was asked to help him get in and out of the studio. The alarm was a mixture of the new and old technologies. On one end at the entrance door to the studio you had computer buttons to push. A certain combination would let you open the door and close the door without any problem. When there was a problem, the other end of this alarm system made itself known. It was attached to the side of the Old Barn

Old Joe Clark, Little Jimmy Dickens, Pee Wee King at the Old Joe Clark Bluegrass Festival in Renfro Valley.

and consisted of bells and whistles that could be heard for a mile around.

Herb had just gone out the door of the studio and was heading for the Old Barn. I stayed behind to lock the doors and set the burglar alarm before following him out. I heard a beep that I thought indicated the alarm was about to go off any second so I rushed back in to turn it off, but I was too late. No sooner had the door closed behind me than the alert whistle began to scream throughout the Valley, telling everyone for a mile or two around that someone was breaking into the building. Well, up rushed the new security guard and there stood poor old Herb at the door with his face hanging out. Herb swears the guard was reaching for his pistol. I didn't know about that because I was locked inside, but I did hear Herb yell, "Hold it, hold it, everything's okay. Pete's in there." When the new security guard asked, "Pete who?" I knew Herb was in trouble. Herb said I could have come out and helped him explain a lot sooner than I did, but I couldn't; I was laughing too hard to get the door open.

The only thing that seemed to be going better than could have been hoped was the *Barn Dance,* the *Jamboree,* the *Sunday Morning Gatherin',* and special events. The Bluegrass Festival, started by Mac Wiseman nineteen years earlier under the direction of the Old Joe

The Parker Brothers at Renfro Valley's *Gospel Jubilee:* Scott Thompson, Dale Ann Bradley, Bobby Sloan, Vester Parker, Virginia Sutton, Ronnie Parker, Jeff Parker, Jim Gaskin, Chubby Howard, Clyde Foley.

Clark family, was still going strong. The Mountain Music Festival came off with flying colors. Headliners were the Bill Sky Family. Others taking part in this three-day event were the Ware Brothers (Chet and Don), George Hunt, the A.L. Phipps Family, Elmer Goodman, Buddy Bell, Buzz Brazeal, Gilbert Thomas, Clyde Davenport, Herstel Flynn and Earl Schaefer. All these folks, well-known in the mountain music circles, joined Renfro Valley's Eversole Brothers, Coy Priddy, Virginia Sutton, Dave Osborn, Old Joe Clark, and Jim and Ruby Ann Gaskin.

The Parker Brothers Bluegrass Band were becoming spotlight stars on the *Barn Dance,* and gospel singer David Marshall was booked for his first appearance. I had never heard of David Marshall until the day Glen Pennington invited me into his office to listen to a tape he had found of David. He had no idea where he was or how to get in touch with him, but he sent word out by way of the grapevine to have David call Renfro Valley as soon as possible. I was sure glad to hear that Glen had talked to him and had set up a date for his appearance on the *Barn Dance.* Now, I liked David Marshall personally and I liked his music, but I did get kind of tired of listening to that tape over and over and over. Every time Glen caught me in his office or could invite me in, we listened to that tape, over and over and over. I later learned that I was just one of many who were called upon to listen to that tape more than a few times. I suppose Glen was trying to convince himself that the effort he was making to get David to our Renfro Valley show was worth it. The audience response he continued to get on our *Moun-*

tain Gospel Jubilee and the *Renfro Valley Barn Dance* seems to say Glen was right again.

I was in the office the day a tape of Dale Ann Bradley fell into Glen's hands. Glen was on the phone immediately, and, just about as quick, Dale Ann drove over from her home in Somerset to meet with him. She was hired on the spot. Dale Ann is one of the people I wish John Lair could have had in his lineup of talent, especially in his *Sunday Morning Gatherin'*, where she fit in so fine. Everyone was sorry she left us at the start of the 1998 season and wished her well with her new touring.

Had all other aspects of the rebuilding of Renfro Valley gone as well as the rebuilding of the *Barn Dance,* the *Jamboree,* and the other shows, all might have been well in Renfro Valley's fiftieth year. The first casualty was Greg Davis. He had become a good friend of mine, and I was real sorry to see him go. Greg returned to the tourism business, and our paths have crossed a couple of times since then. The new vice-president and general manager was Caven Barnett, another native of Madison County and a long-time friend of Ralph Gabbard's. I cannot say how long Barnett was with the company, but he hardly found his way around. I had practically no contact with him during his short stay. The one exception was when I was asked to take him on a walking tour of the Valley to point out all items that might be considered antiques.

As new careers were beginning in Renfro Valley, in Lexington, Kentucky, one was coming to an end—that of the man who had built the Jerry's Restaurant chain from infancy to the corporate giant that it is today. Warren Rosenthal, a native of Paducah, Kentucky, a long-time businessman and resident in the heart of the Bluegrass had sold his stock in the company (a victim of one of those takeovers) and was looking forward to retirement on his beautiful Bluegrass horse farm. But best-laid plans, like horse races, sometimes go astray. It was Freeman Keyes, fifty years earlier, now it was Warren Rosenthal who was being asked to help the financially strapped Renfro Valley organization. Like Keyes, Warren would begin by buying out the interest of two of the owners, Molen and Elkin. But, unlike Keyes, Warren would not be playing the role of the silent partner, even though his entrance into the Valley was without fanfare, and for a while he operated in the shadow of his good friend Ralph Gabbard.

Glen was excited about his new partner. He hadn't told me their company was in so much trouble until Warren Rosenthal had already become involved. It's my understanding that Ralph Gabbard first asked Warren to just look at their game plan, make any suggestions he thought necessary to get them back on track and back on their way to becoming a major attraction. Evidently in addition to some major financing to properly develop the potential of Renfro Valley, a completely new strategy was proposed and adopted. The previous plans were scrapped almost entirely. The construction of the new auditorium was delayed until the following year, and the location was changed from the festival grounds along the creek to a site parallel to the Old Barn where the campsites had been improperly constructed. Campground plans were put aside for the time being. The plan called for tying in the two barn theaters and the museum as a part of a total village.

A change in plans gave new life to the Old Barn. The decision to renovate this historic structure would give a new home to the *Jamboree* just as soon as the new auditorium was completed. Little did we know then that in just a very short time the attendance to our shows would grow to the point that that Old Barn would see more service than it had ever seen in its so-called heyday.

The village plans came off the drawing board and into Renfro Valley soil, not in the festival grounds across the creek as had been planned, but in that spot that had been old barn parking for over fifty years. The little pioneer log cabin and Redbud Schoolhouse were prepared for a move, becoming a part of Renfro Village.

The post office and the country store were moved to Renfro Village. It was an easy move for the post office, just the flag and the shingle, but the country store moved lock, stock, and barrel. Well, actually, there was no stock or barrel, but the lock and everything fastened to it left the old location on U.S. 25 and was moved to its new home between the Old Barn and the New Barn theater.

Footsteps

The big, log museum building was doubled in size with one feature that is still hard for me to believe today—an elevator in Renfro Valley! It replaced the big, wide stairs that came up from the front of the breezeway, although new stairways were installed in the new section. But the elevator completely eliminated the stairs that went up from the hallway inside the broadcast studios and ran up to the old music library and into the museum music room.

I wondered if the changes would disturb the ghost who haunted that big, log building. They had walked those steps for so long. Would that elevator be as hard for them to believe as it was for me? Or maybe they would welcome a ride in their old age? Al Ballinger had heard those footsteps, so had Denver Miller, Old Joe Clark, and the late Russ Fisher. I had heard them a lot of times, as well as every other disk jockey who had worked the morning shift at our small local radio station while it was located in that big log building. As I mentioned before, the studios were located on the first floor below the old pioneer museum, a museum of Civil War rifles, canteens, uniforms, showing the wear and tear and stains of battle. There was one section that featured ladies' old dresses that were displayed along with the trundle bed and a cradle and a coffin.

As I mentioned before, I worked in the museum when I first came to Renfro Valley, but it wasn't until an early morning in January 1958 that I first heard the footsteps coming down the stairs that led from the hall behind the WRVK control room to the museum above. When I first heard them, I went to the foot of the stairs, looked up to where

192

the steps made a turn, and expected to see someone or something coming into view. I would do that many times over the next few years. I don't remember ever hearing the footsteps once I was out in the hall. I don't believe I ever heard them come all the way down, and I don't remember thinking that they were going back up, just coming down. It was a long time before I could hear those steps and not resist going to investigate. Finally, Old Joe, Russ, and I got used to the fact that between 5:00 and 7:00 A.M., always before dawn, we could expect to hear our visitor come down the stairs.

I don't know exactly when I heard the footsteps for the last time, but I can tell you that it was before December 1975. Why that date? Well, I had taken a break from my job earlier that year to travel with the Dolly Parton show, leaving my friend Denver Miller holding down my shift at the mike until I returned. Denver hadn't been there long enough to make friends with the upstairs neighbor and carried a gun to work every morning, just in case.

Well, it was in early morning soon after my return that I saw for the first and last time the person or persons I think might have been making those footsteps. I always enjoyed a good cup of coffee and a cigarette with my music, but sometimes I had to settle for just coffee and music when I would forget to bring matches or a lighter. To make sure that this didn't happen, I had a small hot plate handy in case of emergencies. On this cold December morning I was a few minutes into my program and a puff or two on a freshly lit cigarette when I looked up into the glass that separated the control room from the big studio on the other side. When the lights were off in the studio, the glass in front of me made a pretty good mirror. I was startled to see standing behind me a dark-haired girl in a long white dress or gown with hands stretched out over the hot plate I had forgotten to turn off. It was just a quick glance. I wheeled around expecting to face someone in the room with me, but I found no one there. How long I searched the spot where I thought the girl had stood, I don't know. I suppose the job at hand brought my attention back to the control board and the glass in front of me, and there again I saw the girl as before, but this time there was a child at her side, five or six years old I'd say, dressed in a nightgown, with upstretched arms as if to warm them by the hot plate on the table above its head. As quickly as before, I whirled around to once again stare into an empty room except for a table, a stack of records, a coffee pot, and the red glow of that hot plate.

Before the stairway became a victim of the expansion of the

museum, I went back to those stairs and walked up to where the steps turn left into the old museum, and for the first time I considered the possibility that my ghost may have entered the stairs not from the museum on the left but from the door on my right that led into the old music library where at the time Hans Lindbloom was cataloging thousands of pieces of old sheet music collected over the years by John Lair. I wondered if my woman and child were the subject of one of those old ballads of a tragic romance, maybe even death. I went into the library to talk over this new theory with Hans, and as we talked I looked out over the roof of this second story window into the face of the loveliest girl standing no more than ten feet away. This time her hair was blond; she was dressed in blue jeans and a plaid shirt. Without taking my eyes off of her, I asked Hans to look out the window and tell me if I was seeing what I thought I saw. Hans said, "If you mean the blond in blue jeans out on the roof, that's Mary Talent. She's with the crew that's putting a new roof on the building."

I just wished my dark-haired girl and the child could be as easily explained away. Then maybe I could go back to my usual habit of not really believing in ghosts. It may be a case of which came first, the chicken or the egg. Whether I believed in her before or after telling this story, I can't say. But after the story ran in the December 1989 issue of the *Bugle,* some of those construction workers who were working on the building began to see their own ghost. They even gave it the name of Leonard. Now, down inside I knew they were just pranking, but word was spreading over the Valley—Leonard this, Leonard that, Leonard turned over the trash, Leonard slammed the truck door, Leonard moved the ladder. It was just a bunch of foolishness is what it was, and I didn't like it. The stories were spreading like wildfire, and it was all I could do to put them out. I wasn't going to have no Leonard moving in with my Loreli. Until then I hadn't thought of my woman having a name, but when I did I knew it had to be Loreli.

You don't have to take my word for it. If you ever have the opportunity to talk to Al Ballinger or my disc jockey buddy and now circuit court clerk Denver Miller, they'll tell you that those footsteps kept us company in the early morning hours for many years.

Now and then I'll hear one of the young folks who has been spooked by a noise in the old barn remark, "Well, I guess John is walking again." Well, I can tell them if they ever watched or heard John Lair walk, there would not be a guess about it. John Lair's walk was as unique as most every other thing about him. He walked by scooting, I believe it was his right foot, about every other step or so. The sound of the sole of his shoe scooting on the floor or the gravel could not be mistaken and, if that wasn't enough, you knew it was him by the little whistling noise that he made, not a tune really, just a rapid barrage of notes up and down the scale that made no sense musically speaking but had a purpose according to some of the talent. Lily May used to say that he made these noises to alert anyone he walked up on who just might be talking about him lest he heard something he didn't want to hear and would have to fire the bunch.

On a recent Saturday night following the *Barn Dance* and the *Jamboree*, the last autograph signing was over and the old clock was ticking toward midnight. Connie Hunt and Glenn Thompson were still in the Old Barn discussing the night's performance. A light had been left on in the auditorium at the sound booth. Connie made her way down the aisle to the front of the Barn and turned the light off. On her way back she chose to come up on stage on the left-hand side, which put her near the men's dressing room, where she heard Glenn Thompson's footsteps loud and clear. The only problem was, when she looked across the stage, Glenn Thompson was on the other side. In about a half a second, Connie Hunt was there with him. John Lair wrote someplace that the arrowheads found during construction showed that the Old Barn was either built on an Indian encampment or a battlefield. Just food for thought.

Just a few feet away stands the old museum building that we've talked so much about. A couple of the bookkeepers were recently working late in an office just a few steps from the elevator. More than once they heard the little bell that indicated the elevator was going up or down. They said there was no mistaking this sound as it echoed down the breezeway. I guess that's why I haven't seen anyone burning the midnight oil in that old building lately.

While I'm at it, I might as well tell you about a strange thing that happened on our anniversary show the weekend of November 4, 1991. We put together a special that followed the script of that first performance in 1939. As Jim Gaskin was playing the part of fiddler-comedian Slim Miller, I filled in as emcee and narrator of the first portion of the show. I was seated on a stool up front on the right-hand side of the stage directing the activity out in the spotlight and reading word for word the script just as John Lair had done fifty-one years earlier. I had just introduced Ernie Sowder for his number, and I was watching from my position on stage. Out of the corner of my eye I caught sight of an object that appeared to be maybe three or four loosely bound strands of white string about two to three feet long floating down from out of the darkness above the balcony, moving down and out toward the stage. It traveled slowly enough that I had time to wonder what Ernie was going to do when it suddenly appeared in front of him. Would he duck, or what? But then, suddenly, it disappeared from my view just before reaching the edge of the stage. I sat there trying to figure out what it was that I had seen and where it had gone. A dislodged spider web or something similar, I was thinking, when it reappeared a few feet up above the edge of the stage and began its slow ascent into the darkness from where it had come. I could explain it coming down, whatever it was, but not then and not now can I figure anything that would travel back up the way that it did.

I told a few people about this incident in the next few days, and about a week later Brother Roger Price, Baptist minister and father of Dale Ann Bradley, came looking for me to say that he, too, had seen it from his seat at the back of the theater. He watched it hover over the stage and disappear. Now, I hadn't seen it out over the stage, and he hadn't seen it travel back, but we both saw it come down. I then learned that our light technician, Jan Masters, was videotaping the show from her station in the balcony, and I could hardly wait to watch the show through the lens of her recorder. I watched the pictures of Ernie's performance from top to bottom, side to side, but nothing unusual came into view. Then the musical break came in the song and, being the videographer that Jan was, she moved her recorder off Ernie and onto Bobby Sloan standing at the left and rear of the stage. This had to have been when it happened, either that or whatever it was does not photograph or video. We're still working on an explanation. I have wondered if maybe it was Loreli who just dropped in to see the show, but I don't think she would consider it as a permanent residence. As nice as it is, there is no elevator in the New Barn theater.

The New Guard

Ralph Gabbard made two more early appointments to the Renfro Valley Folks, Jim Tillery and Tom Bennett. Jim was a native of Berea. He had spent a number of years in the broadcast business in Kentucky, Florida, and Oklahoma and was appointed to the position of president and general manager. He was our third general manager in less than a year, and he was short-lived in that role.

Tom Bennett had been project manager for WKYT-TV in Lexington and came on as vice-president of operations. Tom fit right in with the many bulldozers that were on the property, and I always thought he operated in a similar fashion—full speed ahead, don't let anything stand in your way. If a project had a deadline, you could always bet on Tom meeting it with time to spare. No two people were as unlikely friends as Tom Bennett and me. I doubt, considering the great differences in our personalities, that we would have ever given friendship a chance had it not been for the one thing we shared in common—our friend Ralph Gabbard. I was well aware of the fact that on many occasions Tom grew impatient with my slow pace of work and decision making. And, though we had a number of disagreements, I was always treated with respect.

In identifying Warren Rosenthal to me, Glen Pennington told me that he had been chief executive officer at Jerrico, Inc., and was responsible for putting 1,400 Long John Silver's Seafood Shoppes in thirty-seven states and two foreign countries. Well, that was impressive enough, but it was the mention of the sixty-odd Jerry's Restaurants that really got my attention, and that was fifty-nine more than he had to have told me about. Foolish, I suppose, but it kind of made me feel like Warren Rosenthal and Pete Stamper had something in common, and it wasn't our western Kentucky roots, and it wasn't tater pie. No, it was good old strawberry pie, the kind I've only eaten at Jerry's. During my days in the insurance business, we would report in to the office on Fridays and the staff of men I worked with always, without fail, went to lunch at Jerry's. Now, I never had any trouble finding food I loved to eat, and I never paid too much attention to the sign over the door, but when I'm at Jerry's, I never miss the opportunity to have a piece of that good old strawberry pie.

I don't remember if I ever did get around to mentioning that pie to Warren, but I did ask him once how he got into the restaurant business and he told me that it was pure chance. He had graduated from college, gone back to Paducah for a year, and had just interviewed for a job in New York. Not liking the big city, he came back with every intention of making his future in the insurance business. He was on his way to his new job and stopped off in Lexington to say hello to a friend from whom he had rented an apartment while attending the University of Kentucky. His friend, Jerry Lederer, had a small chain of three restaurants named White Taverns and one that bore his name, Jerry's. He told his friend that he was on his way to Louisville to take a job as an insurance agent, whereupon Jerry proposed that he forget about insurance and throw in with him in the restaurant business. He told Jerry he knew nothing about that business and asked what would he do. Jerry said, "You will do like I do." Warren said he listened to the proposal, decided that it sounded pretty good and decided to give it a try. He had watched Jerry getting up at a reasonable hour in the morning and going to the office about 9:00, checking the receipts from the previous day, taking fifty bucks out of petty cash and heading for Keeneland racetrack or the bookies. Warren thought he could learn that job. And he did!

He said this was pretty much the way that he was spending his time until one day when he was making his rounds he stopped in at one of the restaurants. The manager had a tub of kerosene on the back storage room floor and he was cleaning the contents of that tub with a brush. When Warren asked what he was doing, he was told that there was a convention coming up that weekend and that he was making sure that all the exhaust fans were clean and in good working order to lessen the chance that they might break down during the busy part of the week. Warren said he complimented the man on his thoughtfulness, told him he was doing a good job, then went on his way, pleased that he had such a conscientious, loyal manager working for him. A short time later he learned that what the man was really doing was cleaning the transmission of his automobile there on the back room floor. He said then and there that he decided that if he was going to succeed in the restaurant business, he was going to have to learn what every job was really all about. The next day there was no Keeneland. Warren donned an apron and headed for the griddle to learn to do some cooking.

By the way, he tells me you should never mash your hamburger while it cooks. By doing that, you mash out all the flavor, he says. Now he tells me! I have one of those big, old coal stove irons that I place on top of all the hamburgers I cook. I guess I'll keep doing it. If they taste any better than they do right now I wouldn't be able to stand it.

Before our fiftieth season came to a close, CMT, Country Music Television Production Company, hosted by its founder, Stan Hitchcock, turned the lights on in the Old Barn for two performances, one with Stan and the Reno Brothers to be played over the Southern Cable Vision system and the other featuring Renfro Valley's entertainers to be shown over the Nashville-based CMT network. This was to be a big break for Renfro Valley, everyone thought. I never knew what went wrong. As far as I know, this particular show never made it to the air. But others met with better success a little bit later.

The fiftieth anniversary season was coming to a close, but the lights were to stay on in Renfro Valley. Christmas in the Valley was born. Trees and buildings were outlined with thousands of bright Christmas lights. Special shows filled the *Barn Dance* calendar. Campbell Soup, the Christian Appalachian Project and Renfro Valley joined forces for a special *Barn Dance* in support of the Christmas Food Bank. Glen Pennington came to work in the Valley each day around 4 or 5 P.M. He spent most of his time in his office at home. When he hit the Valley, he would usually come by my place at the recording studio to talk to me about the shows and the Gatherin' production and so forth. Glen would like to have played more of a role in the detailed day-by-day operation, but his health would not permit it. When we were alone in the control room on a Saturday afternoon as the singers and band members worked out the musical numbers for the *Sunday Morning Gatherin'*, Glen would share with me things of a personal or private nature. I was only then beginning to learn just how bad his health really was. He only had one kidney, and it was beginning to give him trouble. He held a little pill up one day and said, "This is all that stands between me and a heart attack at any time." But Glen was enjoying this season.

His first year as one of the original partnership of Renfro Valley was coming to a close, a year that had started great, hit on some rough times about midway and was coming back together better with new partners, Ralph and Warren, than he could ever have imagined. Ground had just been broken for the new auditorium. By this time next year there would be a Renfro Village where Santa Claus would be found in every shop. The show schedule was expanding to Tuesday through Sunday. Little did we know that this was going to be Glen's last Merry Christmas on this earth. There would be one more, his last, but it would be sad indeed.

I have a story about this Christmas I'd like to share with you concerning Glen Pennington. I know you've heard stories where the teller begins by saying, "Well, you would have had to have known him to really appreciate it." I guess that might be true in this case. You would have had to have known Glen Pennington to be as amused at this as I am. Glen tried to be as correct as he could be at everything he did. I always liked to hear him tell a joke because he always put in every little detail. He would check and double check, leave no stone unturned. And he, too, crossed every T and dotted every I. Glen always started each conversation with "Say." "Say, what about this?" Kinda like whatever it was had just occurred to him when we knew that whatever he was about to say he had already thought out well in advance. But back to my story. With a satisfied mind, Glen was wrapping up all the details of the Christmas season. He had bought gifts for friends and family, including his business partners, Ralph and Warren. On this particular night, he went to bed satisfied that all was well and nothing else needed his attention. Now, what happened next, probably has happened to many of us at one time or the other. Out of the blue, or in this case out of the black of night, a light went on in his head, and suddenly Glen sat straight up in bed in total panic. His perfect moment went up in a puff. He jumped out of bed and rushed to the phone and promptly dialed the number of Ralph Gabbard in Lexington. Ralph answered, and Glen said, "Say, Ralph, I've just mailed Warren Rosenthal his Christmas gift." Ralph said, "Good." Glen said, "No, it's not good. You see, I sent him a country ham!" After Ralph assured him that everything was okay, Glen said goodnight, hung up, and went back to bed, probably returning to his thoughts concerning the next fifty years of Renfro Valley.

Our fifty-first season got under way with the burial of the time capsule at the foot of the stage in the New Barn theater. Soon after, we buried three old friends—Claud Sweet, Coy Priddy, and Betty Foley Cummins. While we were losing some of the pioneers of the Valley, we were gaining in the number of entertainers, management, and employees. It seemed there for a while that we had about three people to every job. Renfro Valley Folks became the second largest employer in Rockcastle County, second only to the county school system.

The Tuesday and Wednesday night shows were to fail temporarily. Renfro Valley broke the ice in the star concert events by bringing in *Hee Haw*'s country gospel entertainer, Lulu Roman, for performances in June 1990.

A new feature writer for the *Bugle* began a monthly article entitled "A Backward Glance." She was Kathy McCracken, a native of Rockcastle County. Kathy would soon become our editor and hold that position until her untimely death in 1994. She doubled as Warren's secretary after he replaced Jim Tillery. She taught him most everything he knows about the history of Renfro Valley, he says.

Christian Tours honored us with an invasion of Renfro Valley with the largest tour group we had ever seen, a total of twenty-three buses and 1,100 people and, with our other guests, this made for a mighty big weekend in Renfro Valley.

As the song says, "What a Difference a Day Makes." We never knew just when the decisive day came, but because of his failing health, Glen Pennington, once again, true to form, went about putting his house in order. He called upon his partners, Ralph Gabbard and Warren Rosenthal, to buy his share of the company, a transaction that took place without public knowledge, as Glen retained his role as vice-president and entertainment director. But the Christmas season would not be the merry one of Christmases past. Gift buying would be left to his lovely wife, Vivian. My last conversation with Glen was during the taping of our *Sunday Morning Gatherin'* radio program that December. He informed me that he was going into the hospital for a few days. I remember asking him if it was serious, and, after a pause, a pause he was famous for, he said, "extremely serious."

The February 1991 issue of the *Bugle* reserved for itself page 13 to commemorate its forty-seventh anniversary, giving the front page over to the death of one of the Valley's most devoted friends and admirers. Glen died on February 4 at Central Baptist Hospital in Lexington. His involvement in Renfro Valley in one way or the other spanned a total of forty-eight years. Warren and Ralph dedicated the New Barn in Glen's honor the following year. Miss Vivian's love for the Valley and her memories of Glen are still evident. Each showtime finds her selling our programs to the audience, and she is the first to greet you at the *Sunday Morning Gatherin'*.

At the close of the article announcing Glen's death it was noted that Ralph Gabbard had announced that Pete Stamper would become the new director of entertainment. During Glen's stay in the hospital I had time to consider the possibility that I might be offered the job, and even though I'm sure I would have been disappointed had I not been asked, I had decided to turn it down if and when the offer came. The one thing that would most qualify me for the job I knew would be the one thing that would give me the most trouble. As a veteran entertainer and a longtime member of the *Renfro Valley Barn Dance*, I thought I knew the kinds of shows we should continue to do. But directing my fellow entertainers, especially when their views might not jive with mine, would be difficult for me, as I needed their respect and friendship more than the company recognition. And, too, my involvement with the operation of Renfro Valley for more years than I care to admit had begun to take its toll and to burn me out a little. I was beginning to look forward to the day when I could take it easy.

When Ralph Gabbard called, I found it a little harder to turn down the position than I had expected, but I stuck to my guns and told him that I was turning the offer down and told him why, just to listen to him shoot down every excuse that I gave him. So, I promised him that I would think it over for a few days. I began to think less of whether I could do the job and more about the person that would be appointed, whether they would know what was involved in running our *Jamboree* and *Barn Dance*. I guess I wanted the job more than I realized, and with the prospect that we might end up with someone who would do our show harm, I called Ralph and told him that if his offer was still good, I would take it. He promised to come to my aid if needed but would give me a completely free hand as long as I did not do anything completely off the wall. I felt sure I was not about to do that.

Well, I saw right away that I was going to have my hands full. The 1991 show schedule was unprecedented, even to this day: Tuesday through Sunday stage shows and forty special events ranging all the way from Easter Egg Hunts and Quilting Bees to Country Music Jams and Country Cooking Fairs. Every weekend, a special event.

Richard Anderkin of the *Mt. Vernon Signal* was credited with editing our *Bugle,* but Susan Mitchell and Cathy McCracken, feature writers, were doing most of the labor on our little newspaper.

I left my footprints in a place or two in Renfro Valley over the years, one I've mentioned already, and that's bringing Bun Wilson to our stage. And I'm mighty proud of the part that I played in bringing one of the finest female comedians to this or any other stage. Her name is Betty York. When Betty came to my attention, she was not what we would call a professional entertainer. She had been entertaining before some of the civic clubs in her area, but I saw a video of one of her performances and right away recognized a delivery and a knowledge of comedy material that is seldom seen in performers with her limited experience. For some time we had been making an effort to find a female comedian. We ran ads in our *Bugle* and other newspapers and went as far as to have a special performance one year looking for that right person. When I saw the amateur video of one of Betty's civic club performances, I knew our search was over.

Another footprint I'm proud to leave has to do with the country store. My role as entertainment director had little to do with that other than that it may have given me the opportunity to sell the idea to management. In June 1990, I spent a little time with Justin Tubb at Fanfare in Nashville, and we talked about the record shop down on Broadway that his dad had made famous. I remembered the times I had gone in and looked at the display of pictures of the famous Grand Ole Opry recording stars, thumbed through rows upon rows of records of all kinds and listened to live music in the little studio in back of the Record Shop. Justin told me that he had a new store opening in Gatlinburg and had been thinking about Renfro Valley.

During the next few months I began to think about Renfro Valley with its own record shop. As the Old Country Store was being fitted to its new foundation at Renfro Village, I began to imagine it as the record shop I saw for Renfro Valley. I made an appointment with the village shop manager and told him about the idea, and he informed me that a decision had been made to turn the building into a general store or a variety store. He said that more than likely some tapes and records would be sold someplace in the store. I left his office with every intention of just forgetting it, but something kept nagging at me. So my next stop was with the general manager, Jim Tillery. He told me about the same thing, except he assured me that there would be a little section set aside for cassette tapes. Soon after that I had reason to talk to Jane Thorne, who at the time headed up the accounting department. I had found her to be one who listened to an idea or a problem even if she was not in a position to help in any way. I tried to get across to her the importance of this being a music store and nothing else, and I believe I succeeded, for she said she thought the little log cabin could be made available for what I had in mind. I told her that I thought that would be much better than just a corner in another shop but that I felt that it should have bigger quarters if they were ever available.

It was a few days later at a meeting with Ralph Gabbard at his office in Lexington when we discussed my role as entertainment director and the directions our shows were to take. As always, the conversation included an overall look at Renfro Valley. Something in that conversation prompted me to mention my idea of a record shop in the old store building. I told him my idea of decorating similar to the Ernest Tubb Record Shop with old album covers that I had collected over the years. And keeping the little studio in back of the store as part of our history rather than taking it out as had been planned. As I talked he was making notes. I wasn't sure if it was concerning our conversation or something else that he had remembered, and I told him I thought the store should include a special section for Renfro Valley tapes, music of our current entertainers and those from our archives. When I was finished, his comment was, "That's interesting." That was just about it. The following week I received a copy of a letter that he had mailed to Jim Tillery detailing the things we had talked about in his office and asking Jim to look into the possibility of turning the country store into a record shop. In no time at all it seemed, Jim, Tom Bennett, and I were in Nashville learning everything we could about the record, tape, and CD business. The managers at the Ernest Tubb Record Shop gave us full run of the place and answered all the questions that we knew to ask. I wish I could say that I always knew the store would be as successful as it has been, but I can't do that. I think I was aware of the market for our nostalgia tapes maybe better than anyone because of the *Gatherin'* tapes I had been selling on Sunday morning for a number of years. But, mostly, I just wanted Renfro Valley to have its own music store, the kind I always visited when I went to Nashville.

Ever since the opening of the store, the casts of the *Barn Dance* and *Jamboree* shows have left the stage after the shows and come to

1995 autograph session. Photo by Greg Perry.

the music store to sign autographs, hug, and howdy. One of the reasons the store may have been the success that it was from the beginning was its first manager. Her name is Linda Ray, and she has an uncontrollable appetite for digging her heels into any job she is doing. She set out to do research on all old music, where and how it might be obtained and corresponding with folks who had requested certain items that we didn't have. It wasn't too long until we could honestly say, "If we don't have it, we'll get it, and if we can't get it, it can't be got." Terry Jones has been store manager for many years now and continues to upgrade the record shop in every way possible, keeping it a place of pride for all of us entertainers.

A "too good to refuse" offer to Jim Tillery by a broadcast station in northern Kentucky again left us without a general manager. Warren Rosenthal came out of semi-retirement in his stead and filled in for a few weeks until Ralph Gabbard appointed Dean L. Henricksen to that post.

The Changing of the Guard

I heard through the grapevine later in the year that there was to be another change in ownership. Once again, Warren Rosenthal would replay the role of Freeman Keyes and, figuratively speaking, turn the investment over to Ralph Gabbard and some other parties for a dollar. Just before the opening of the fifty-third season there was a meeting at Old Joe's Restaurant of entertainers, management, and owners. The announcement was made public. Warren explained that he was bowing out to enjoy his retirement. He said he would be paying us a visit from time to time and would continue in an advisory role but that Ralph Gabbard would be steering the Valley on into the future. Ralph took the podium and expressed his pleasure at having the opportunity to take Renfro Valley into the next fifty years and pleaded for our help and cooperation. Then we were asked to bite the bullet and take a 5 percent cut in pay for a little while in order to give the new owners some breathing room and time to restructure bank loans. Everyone seemed to be willing to go along with the cut for a time as they considered Ralph a friend in need. But as it turned out, his needs were for more than just room to breathe. Something had gone wrong, as it has a habit of doing, even in the best-laid plans. Ralph and his new associates couldn't come up with the "dollar" or the ability to handle the debt. In fact, a short time later, it was he who would find it necessary to bow out completely as far as his financial involvement was concerned. Ralph Gabbard remained a friend and advisor to Renfro Valley Incorporated until his untimely death at the age of fifty in 1996. Warren Rosenthal, who had never heard of John Lair or Renfro

Valley before the summer of 1989, was now its sole owner. His involvement for the prior three years had been extensive, especially in the building of the new village and remodeling the lodge. But, as I mentioned earlier, his partners, Ralph Gabbard and Glen Pennington, were usually at the head of the table as far as the entertainers and staff were concerned.

A little way into the new season, Warren showed up one day wearing a bright plaid shirt, the traditional uniform of Renfro Valley Folks. Everyone noticed and most commented in one way or the other, but I think we all missed the significance of that shirt. It was telling us that Keeneland was going to have to wait a little longer. Once again, Warren Rosenthal was stepping up to the griddle to do some cooking.

All those weekly special events that proved unfruitful were dropped from our 1992 calendar, trading quantity for quality. More time and effort went into the ones that remained while at the same time we went outside the Valley for some special appearances. The *Renfro Valley Barn Dance* and *Jamboree* musicians joined with the Lexington Philharmonic in performing "Country with the Pops," which was repeated for a couple of years. Renfro Valley also joined forces with Eastern Kentucky University talent for some specials that were staged on their campus and in our New Barn auditorium. This resulted in our discovery of Heather Carrico, an extremely talented young student who joined our *Jamboree* cast and will be remembered as one of our most popular vocalists.

But it was our own musical production that was added to our Christmas in the Valley celebration that took the spotlight. I would gladly lay claim to this idea if I could. The first I heard of it was at a meeting of the department heads when it was presented to me for my approval. Evidently it had been discussed in advance of my arrival, for it seemed that everyone was wholeheartedly in favor. Tom Bennett pressed me for my thoughts on it. I begged for a little time to think it over. I did present my doubts about it. I wondered about those folks who had driven for miles and miles expecting to see a country music show just to end up listening to an hour and a half of Christmas music, and I wondered about the acting ability of our Renfro Valley talent, whether we would be up to taking on a complicated script. I never was fully convinced that the Christmas production would be the least bit successful. But it seemed I was the only one who had any doubts at all. Kathy McCracken, *Bugle* editor, who because of her religious beliefs did not observe the Christmas holidays, still thought the Christ-

1993 Christmas in the Valley.

mas production would be great for the Valley. Her help in writing that first script went a long way toward ensuring its success.

It was at a luncheon given for the Renfro Valley employees in the Red Barn that Warren walked up and asked me what we were going to do about the Christmas show. I had prepared an answer that I thought would emphasize just how serious my doubts were. I told him we could only do it if we had no less than seven rehearsals and possibly as many as nine. These rehearsals were going to cost a pretty penny, but I believed they were necessary. Warren thought a minute, then said, "You had better get at it, hadn't you?" Needless to say, the Christmas production along with the other activities has made Christmas in the Valley the most successful special event in our sixty-year history. The newest production that was presented in the 1996 season was written by Jim Gaskin, Connie Hunt, Betty Lou York, and me, based on an idea by our stage manager and director, Warren "Ziegfeld" Rosenthal, and really did take us another step into acting and production. Its continued success allows me to make that statement.

I can't help but look forward to our last night of the season with

Warren congratulates Pete on receiving the Boo Boo Award.

mixed emotions. We need the break, and we always end with our big award show and dinner. Now this is the one time when we play "Hollywood and Nashville" and give out awards for the best male this and female that. I've been lucky once or twice and was able to take something home to hang on the wall. The award that sets us apart from the others is what was called the "Boo Boo Award," a trophy for the one who makes the biggest blunder during the year. I had always missed that honor, but when it was discontinued, I didn't mind that either.

Then came the night I was emceeing the *Jamboree* show. We had a guest performer I knew well, a young man who had been on our show a half dozen times in the past; his name was John Austin McDaniel from down in western Kentucky near Kentucky Lake country. He's a good entertainer and we always look forward to his appearance. As he and I were waiting in the wings for the act on stage to finish, someone there was talking about an appearance that a hot country artist was making at Rupp Arena in Lexington that very night. I suppose I had that in the back of my mind as I ran on stage to introduce our guest. Without a second's hesitation, I walked to the mike and said, "Folks, I have the pleasure to introduce a fine entertainer who is paying us a visit tonight. Would you all make welcome now, John Michael Montgomery." Well, the house broke out in applause, and the acts on stage fell over laughing, and poor John Austin McDaniel walked on stage looking at me with a question I couldn't answer because I did not realize until I was told backstage what I had said. This was in the spring of the year; by the end of the season I had lived it down, I thought. I don't know if a vote was taken, but everyone agreed that this warranted the re-establishment of the "Boo Boo Award."

I can't say that the 1993 season began in my favor entirely. A decision had been made by Dean Henricksen, the then CEO of Renfro Valley, to dismantle the *Jamboree* as we had known it for four years and rebuild it giving it an entirely new image. It was the format for rebuilding that I strongly disagreed with. The show had been a traditional country music comedy show, just about dividing the hour and a half between comedy and vocals. The number of songs usually ranged from twelve to fourteen. The new format was to do away entirely with the comedy, increasing the number of vocals to the mid-twenties. The only time a lineup like this would ever work is when there is a star in the spotlight with as many hit songs to their credit. This plan was going forward in spite of my objection, which put me between a rock and a hard place. Of course, resigning was never an option. I couldn't walk away from the first major problem that I had to face. And I had just been honored with the title of vice-president, and I wanted to enjoy that for a while longer. Neither could I pretend that it was my idea or even that I was going along, for a lot of the talent knew better. At the first rehearsal in the presence of management and talent, I announced that I was stepping out of the role of director on this project and that Dean Henricksen would have full control. I received no satisfaction in the fact that the *Jamboree* suffered quite a lot in the beginning, as I knew it would. Fortunately, Warren was out front watching and listening and intervened by putting me back in the lineup as a comedian and later as emcee and followed with the addition of Betty Lou York with her great comedy.

Bun Wilson laughingly still accuses me of instigating the whole thing just to get rid of him. I point out to him that if I did, it didn't work; we're right back working our magic along with Betty Lou York Saturday afternoons in the fastest comedy show I have ever been a part of. We're given thirty minutes, we take thirty-five and we want forty-five. It's my favorite performance of the week.

I stayed on as director of entertainment a little longer than I thought I might when I took the job, but a little less than I later planned. At the close of the 1992 season, I decided 1995 was to be my last year. Early in 1993 I began to have second thoughts. In an interview with Rita Stuart Spears for her book *Remembering the Ozark Jubilee,* Rita closed the questioning by asking me about my future plans. This question came as a surprise, as did my answer. It was the first time I had put into words a desire to write, to make guest appearances, and to travel to some places I had always wanted to visit. I have since found that doing these things wasn't so important as having the freedom to do them if I so desired. Continuing to entertain was always at the top of my list of things to do as well as my work with the Renfro Valley *Gatherin'* production. There were some conflicts of ideas concerning entertainment that had begun to surface at the time that made my resignation a little awkward. They had little to do with my decision, but I knew it might appear that they had all to do with my stepping aside. The truth was that at that stage of my life I was not up to taking on the demands of a Renfro Valley on the grow. I sought the help of Jane Thorne once again. I knew she would hear more of what I had on my mind than just the fact that I was turning over my duties as director. She saw to it that the right person or persons heard my request, and I'm proud to say my wishes were more than met to my satisfaction.

It took me the better part of the 1994 season to get used to the idea that they could operate without me. I was kinda hoping, I think, that Connie Hunt would find it necessary to call me up for advice two or three times a day, but it seemed her musical background and her years with other departments in the company had more than qualified her for the task at hand. Unlike the days when it seemed there were three people to every job, there are now three jobs for every person, but most have a lot of experience with Renfro Valley entertainment under their belts and most are up to the challenge.

A Family Affair

As I have mentioned and you will hear a time or two each time you're here, the Renfro Valley Folks are a family, and more and more we're becoming families within that family. When Scott Thompson joined his dad, Glenn, in the *Jamboree* Band, it set the stage for one of the most visible families we've had. Glenn played the lead guitar; Scott was at the drums. Retha, Glenn's wife, was the long-time sound technician for our shows, and when Scott married Coon Creek Girl Jennifer Wrinkle, every member of the Thompson family was a member of the Renfro Valley family.

One of the largest families we ever had was in the late seventies and early eighties when the Glenn Bullock clan took over our ticket sales and concession stands. And the Cromers, Delbert and his son Delbert Jr., and James and his son Bubby, were all maintenance crews and security for twenty-five years or more.

The Parker family began to put down roots in the Valley in the early sixties; Vester Parker was banjo picker with the Bluegrass Drifters. When Vester's brothers and sons came on the scene, the Parker Brothers Band was born. The band was made up of Vester, his brothers James and Ronnie, and Vester's sons Mike and Jeff. There was an increase in this family while they were at Renfro Valley when Ronnie married banjo-picker Jan Cummins. For many years, seldom was there a time when there was not at least one Parker in our group of musicians.

The Old Joe Clark family has been prominent in Renfro Valley for a good many years. Joe and Jean raised four young 'uns. Though

The *Barn Dance* and *Jamboree* Band. Back: Bobby Sloan, Chubby Howard, Jack "Doc" Lewis. Middle: Jeff Watson, Don Gulley, Mark Laws, Bill Morris, Glenn Thompson. Front: Pam Perry Clark.

Butch, Sarah, and George were not musicians, they were the subject of many of John Lair's *Gatherin'* scripts when they were young. Joe's young son Terry was added to Joe's stage act in 1969, first as chauffeur and straight man. As his musical talents on the banjo began to develop, Joe began to put Terry in the spotlight more and more.

The family team of Don and Steve Gulley was increased by number and talent when Steve and Debbie Shipley became man and wife.

Donna Dailey joined our Renfro Valley family in 1989 as vocalist on the *Barn Dance* and soon became a leader in our sales department while moving to the *Jamboree* as vocalist and master of ceremonies. Her sister, Connie Hunt, joined Renfro Valley around 1990, taking over the ticket office and moving through various departments before settling down to her duties as vice-president of entertainment. Connie

Barn Dance and *Jamboree* cast of 1992. Front: Pete Stamper, Scott Thompson, Don Jeff Watson, Carrie Stone, Susan Tomes, Chuck Johnson, Jim Gaskin, Donna Faye. Sutton. Fourth row: Donna Dailey, Debbie Gulley, Jeff Parker, Dale Ann Bradley, Isaacs (the Chicken Man).

Gulley, Old Joe Clark, Ernie Sowder, Clyde Foley, Chubby Howard. Second row:
Third row: Steve Gulley, Ethan Eversole, Eric Eversole, Vester Parker, Virginia
Betty Lou York, Bobby Sloan. Back row: Glenn Thompson, Bun Wilson, Jerry

1998 Christmas Show cast picture. From left: Connie Hunt (entertainment direc-
Sloan, Mark Laws, Jerry Isaacs, Susan Tomes, Craig Wells, Kaleesa Robinson,
Roger Drake, Greg Jones, Glenn Thompson, Betty Lou York, Bun Wilson, Jane

is responsible for developing the headliner concerts and for the continued improvements in our shows. For three years, brother Jeff took
command of our recording studio and sound duties. It was Jeff who
handled the recording of the many tapes produced each year by the
Renfro Valley entertainers. The Hunt family are natives of Renfro
Valley, having grown up at the head of Renfro Creek. Donna has told
me many times about her grandfather Gustafson's big, old barn, where
John Lair used to hold his play-parties when he was growing up in
the Valley.

The Blairs, Jeff and John, worked behind the scenes. Jeff is our
operations director, and John is in charge of security and personnel.
And the Thornes: Jane is now executive vice-president and general
manager; her daughter Kelley is usher; and her husband, Bill, is the
director of food services. Both Jane and Bill had worked for Warren
in his Jerrico days. Just recently Bill and his crew fed 1,100 Boarding-

tor), Jim Gaskin, Donna Dailey, Terry Clark, Jeff Watson, Pam Perry, Bobby
Debbie Gulley, Steve Gulley, Justin Rogers, Don Gulley, Billy Keith, Tasha Harris,
Thorne (executive vice president and general manager, Pete Stamper (Santa).

house guests on a Saturday evening while we played to four full houses
in the Old Barn on a Saturday afternoon and two full houses Saturday night, plus a headliner star was performing to two sold-out crowds
in the New Barn. The campgrounds were full with the overflow parked
across the creek. Both big parking lots were filled with cars, trucks,
and vans. The bus parking was bulging with a total of fifteen tour buses.
Now, this was not your typical Renfro Valley weekend, but they are
becoming more frequent all the time. The 1998 season had thirty-four
special attractions scheduled, just about one every week, which, along
with our regular shows, provided more variety than ever before.

   With headliners such as Carl Hurley, Don Williams, Ray Price,
Patty Loveless, the Oak Ridge Boys, Roy Clark, Brenda Lee, and Loretta
Lynn, excitement, advance sales, and pride of all who are a part of
Renfro Valley runs high.

In Closing

A quote from the past comes to mind right here and it goes something like this, in fact it goes exactly like this: "Just imagine what this place could be if the right person ever gets ahold of it." Now if I'd heard that just once, twice, or three times, it would be entirely out of place here. But I've heard it said so many times from so many that it would be an injustice to this effort to leave it out. I have given it a lot of thought and, in my judgment as a long-time entertainer in spite of my limited business experience, I don't believe there will ever be anyone more right for Renfro Valley than the man who now has ahold of it, Warren Rosenthal.

Now, I suppose there's a lot of folks who've been wondering how I would handle this part of the story. Most, I'm sure, knew I would not be fool enough to bite the hand that feeds me, but I like to think that I'm smart enough to write about my Renfro Valley without heaping praise where it is not deserved. I'm not saying we have a perfect little Valley in every respect for every entertainer and every employee all the time. There will be those who will experience difficulties that for one reason or another they will not be able to work their way through and so will leave us. But that's the way it's always been, and I suppose that's the way it will always be. Now and then I run into old friends who have left us for a variety of reasons and in most cases they look back on their Renfro Valley experience with fond memories. This too is the way it's always been, and I hope always will be.

It's no longer the "valley where time stands still." There's a beautiful village complete with pond and grist mill, a city hall with a clock

Warren "Ziegfeld" Rosenthal helping to direct the new production of the Christmas show.

Warren Rosenthal, pleased with his accomplishments, strolls the walk just outside the Village.

in its tower, a post office, a restaurant, the aroma from the candy cooking in the candy store, and a number of craft shops where you can browse for hours. There is the John Lair Theater that takes you back to the very beginning by way of actual recordings of that time, synchronized to a life-size robotic replica of Mr. Lair; the old log school-house that played a role in the beginning of the Renfro Valley settlement; and the new Freedom Church, a site of special gospel performances by and for our village guests; the big log building doubled in size but with the appearance of time-worn beauty; the Lodge restaurant, restored to its original appearance with a state-of-the-art modern kitchen; the little log "tourist cabins" improved with modern heat, air-conditioning, and bath, doubling the original size but keeping that rustic look and feel that returning honeymooners remember. The Old Barn is no longer hot in summer and cold in winter; new theater seats replaced the old hard wooden chairs, but care was taken to keep the stage looking much as it did at the very beginning. While outside there's no indication that any change has been made at all. Concrete walks wind their way through grass, trees, and gardens of flowers within the village. A lot of cooking has gone on in this little wide place in the road but, through it all, it's remembered, "Never mash the burger."

Should Dolly decide to honor us with another visit one day soon, we could and would promise her the red carpet treatment, but I'm afraid I could no longer assure her that her mid-day arrival would go unnoticed because of the lack of guests as I was able to do twenty years ago. With our dozen plus shows a week along with everything else the Valley now has to offer, we haven't had to have a coon dog sale day in quite a while.

The future of a vibrant Renfro Valley and the sound of country music reverberating through the hills are most assuredly to live long after those responsible for ownership and management and the entertainers and musicians who grace these stages have long gone to the big barn above. Speaking as an entertainer, I salute those men of dreams and schemes, of fame and fortune, who have bartered, borrowed, bought and built and who have kept the footlights burning on the best little stage in entertainment, a stage rooted in the fun and frolic of both big city vaudeville and the home-made music of the mountains, a stage that looks out over the very best audience an entertainer could ever ask for.

Renfro Valley Village today.

In 1957 John Lair published a little booklet entitled *Renfro Valley: Then and Now.* Of its forty-six pages, thirty-nine were devoted to the years and events that led up to opening night at Renfro Valley; only the last seven pages were given over to a brief summary of Renfro Valley's first eighteen years. This seems to confirm a truth in an old saying I've heard all my life, "Getting there is half the fun." Let me add that if you don't make it, it's all of it.

I recall something John Lair said many, many years ago and proudly repeated more than a few times over the past fifty-nine years. It is as true today as it's ever been: "At Renfro Valley we have the kind of fun on Saturday night we don't have to be ashamed of on Sunday morning."

To the movers and shakers who will tomorrow hold the deed to my town, please be mindful of the footprints left by those who went before you. And to you nomads of music and misfits of mirth who in your pursuit of happiness are turned by whatever force to my Renfro

Valley, you may be the most fortunate of all. For there may come a time when, in addition to the fun and frolic, your Renfro Valley experience could help bring you a little of that fame and fortune you so eagerly seek. Just be mindful of the fact that fame and fortune in any amount comes to but a few. In the end, it's the fun and the frolic that make it all worthwhile.

Appendix
Sixty Years of Renfro Valley Talent

It's said that there are no small parts. This applies to every player who has cut grass, swept floors, sold tickets, wrote letters, cooked and served food, or tooted the Renfro Valley horn in any way. Without their participation, this milestone could not have been reached. The stars whose names we record here would not have shone as brightly without the help of many others.

Jim Alford, vocal
Virgil "Slim" Alfrey
Paul Alwine, vocal
Betha Amburgey, vocal
Irene Amburgey, vocal
Opal Amburgey, vocal
Charlie Arnette, vocal
Daisy Mae Arnette, vocal
Bob Autry, vocal

Buddy Bain, vocal
Bob Baker, vocal
Jess Baker, vocal
Wade Baker, vocal
Linville Ball, gospel vocal
Al Ballinger, vocal, emcee
Earl Barnes
Wanda Barnett, fiddle, vocal
Eddie Beckley, vocal

Elsie Behrens, vocal
Jerry Behrens, vocal
Janet Benge, banjo
Elmer Bentley, gospel vocal
Peggy Bentley, gospel vocal
Phillip Bentley, gospel vocal
Michelle Birkby, fiddle
Guy Blakeman, fiddle
Mel Blose, vocal
Blue Bonnet Girls (Florence, Lily, Sylvia), vocal
Shorty Bradford, vocal
Dale Ann Bradley, vocal
Ray Brandenburg
Red Brigham, vocal
Sue Brock, vocal
Kathy Brown, vocal
Arlene Bullock
Gwen Bullock

223

Jerri Bullock, vocal
Linda Bullock, vocal
Jackie Burdine, vocal
Pete Burdine, vocal
Jethro Burns, comedy, vocal
Dwight Butcher, emcee
Jerry Byrd, steel

Curt Caldwell, bass
Betty Callahan, vocal
Ginger Callahan, banjo, vocal
Clara Callaway, vocal
Coleida Callaway, vocal
Sudie Callaway, banjo, vocal
Rick Campbell
Amy Carlon, keyboard, vocal
Swannie Cornett, guitar
Heather Carrico, vocal
Charlie Carrol, vocal
Cash Quartet, vocal
Chaney Sisters, vocal
Donny Chastene
Mark Christopher
Ramona Chruch, banjo, vocal
Terry Clark, banjo, vocal
Manuel D. Clark (Old Joe), comedy, banjo, vocal
Phil Clem, vocal
Gene Cobb, comedy
Norma Coffey, vocal
Elezabeth Coleman, vocal
Collins Family
Bill Collins, vocal
Garnet Collins, vocal
Herschel Collins, comedy
Clay Colson, vocal
Randall Conn
Ernie Lee Cornelison, vocal
John Cosby, vocal
Tommy Covington, stell
Donna Cox, vocal
Red Creech, guitar, vocal

Sharon Creech, vocal
Dixie Lee Criswell, vocal
Sally Jo Criswell, vocal
Jan Cummins, banjo, vocal
Kelli Cummins, vocal

Donna Dailey, vocal, emcee
Lloyd Davidson, vocal
Roy Davidson, vocal
Ches Davis, comedy
Lynn Davis, vocal
Melissa Dean, vocal
Junior Defore, mandolin
Judy Dell, vocal
Barbara DeMott, producer
John DeMott, producer
Jo DePew, vocal
Little Jimmy Dickens, vocal
Dick Dickerson, steel
Jean Dickerson, vocal
Judy Dickerson, vocal
Roger Drake, keyboard
Tommy Dunsmore, vocal
Buddy Durham, fiddle
Charlie Durham, fiddle

Clay Eager, vocal
Darrell Edister, guitar
Charles Elza (Kentucky Slim), comedy
Bob England, steel
Hank England, vocal, emcee
Jerry Evans
Eric Eversole, fiddle, vocal
Ethan Eversole, banjo, vocal

Hazel Farmer, vocal
Marie Farmer, vocal
Miss Bess Farmer, organ, vocal
Tillman Farthing, bass
Donn Faye, vocal
Jo Nell Fisher, vocal

Russ Fisher, guitar, vocal
Patty Flye, accordian, vocal
Harold Flynn, steel
Clyde Foley, guitar
Clyde "Red" Foley, vocal
Howard "Nick" Foley, vocal, emcee
Whitey Ford (the Duke of Paducah), comedy, emcee
Mildred Frederick, vocal
Harold French
Mike French, vocal
Bill Ferguson, bass

Billy Gabbard, vocal
Bobby Gabbard, vocal
Pam Gadd, banjo, vocal
Jim Gaskin, fiddle, emcee
Ruby Ann Gaskin, vocal
Morris Gaskins, vocal
Troy Lee Gentry, vocal
Troy Gibbs, bass
Jeannie Gibson, vocal
Lonnie Glosson, harmonica
Millie Good (Girls of the Golden West), vocal
Dolly Good (Girls of the Golden West), vocal
Georgiana Goode, vocal
Dick Graham, vocal
Valerie Graham, vocal
Billy Grimes, banjo
Ralph Grubbs, mandolin
Debbie Shipley Gulley, vocal
Don Gulley, vocal
Steve Gulley, bass, vocal

Homer Haines, comedy, vocal
Don Harper, guitar
Granny Harper, comedy, fiddle, vocal
Tasha Harris, vocal

Arlis Harris (Jubilee Four), gospel vocal
Pauling Harris (Jubilee Four), gospel vocal
Charlie Harrison, comedy, vocal, emcee
Ray Harrison
"Birdseed" Haycraft, vocal
Randy Hayes, guitar
Steve Hays
Ruth Helgerson (Travis Twins), vocal
Ruby Helgerson (Travis Twins), vocal
Mary Hensley, vocal
Wayne Hensley (Hensley Brothers), gospel vocal
Allen Hensley (Hensley Brothers), gospel vocal
Freddie Hensley (Hensley Brothers), gospel vocal
Red Herron, fiddle
Roy "Shorty" Hobbs, comedy
Grady Hockett, vocal
Fairley Holden, vocal
Jack Holden, vocal
Hank Holland, vocal
Ray Holliday, vocal
Chubby Howard, steel
Dean Huddleston, mandolin, vocal
Ricca Hughes, comedy
Mary Humes (Prairie Songbirds), vocal
Margie Humes (Prairies Songbirds), vocal
Danny Hurst, vocal
Shirley Hurst, vocal
Betty Jean Hurt, vocal

Boyd Ingram, vocal
John Ireson, vocal

Jerry Isaacs, comedy

Lucky Jenkins
Chuck Johnson, vocal
Greg Jones, steel
Phyllis Jones, vocal
Judie Jones, vocal
Julie Jones, vocal
Jostus Sisters, vocal

Annie Kaser, banjo
Curley Kerkner, vocal
Gerald King, vocal
Marshall "Slim" King, vocal
Jake Kissinger, dobro, vocal
Violet Koehler, vocal
Billy J. Kramer, drums
Kathy Kuhn, fiddle

Arthur Lakes
Freddie Langdon, fiddle, vocal
Daisy Lange, fiddle, vocal
Cathy Lavendar, vocal
Mark Laws, drums, vocal
Lily May Ledford, banjo, vocal
Rosey Ledford, vocal
Susan Ledford, vocal
Jack "Doc" Lewis, steel, sax
Margaret Lillie (A'nt Idy), comedy
Betty Linn, fiddle
Charlie Linville
Margie Linville, fiddle
Eller Long, comedy
Bill Lovern
Bee Lucas, fiddle

Lilly Mack
Luke Mack
Ralph Marcum, fiddle
"Sleepy" Marlin, fiddle
David Marshall, gospel vocal
Renee Marshall, vocal
Emory Martin, banjo

Linda Lou Martin, fiddle, steel, vocal
Tony Martin, vocal
Ronnie Matthews, vocal
Roger McLure
Miss Ruth McFerron, organ
Buck McKenzie, vocal
Jack McNew, kazoo, vocal
Gary Meredith
Linda Meredith, vocal
Ty Meredith, vocal
Jo Midkiff, vocal
Wayne Midkiff, fiddle, vocal
Homer "Slim" Miller, fiddle, comedy
Plaz Mobley, vocal
Sonny Morgan, steel
Bill Morris, keyboard
Mountain Harmony, gospel vocal
Ray Mulkey, vocal
Shug Mulkey, vocal
Curly Mullican
Connie Mullican, vocal
Mulligan Brothers
Harry Mullins (Little Clifford), comedy

"Country" Charlie Napier, vocal, emcee
Jay Neece, fiddle
Leanne Neeley, clog dancer

Molly O'Day, vocal
Dave Osborn, vocal
David Osborne, vocal
Owen Sisters, vocal

James Parker, bass, vocal
Jeff Parker, mandolin, vocal
Mike Parker, bass
Randall Parker, vocal
Rhuel Parker, fiddle, vocal
Rob Parker, vocal

Ronnie Parker, vocal
Vester Parker, banjo, vocal
Bobby Pennington, drums
Glen Pennington, bass, vocal
Penny Perry, banjo
"J" Perkins, vocal
Mary Lou Perkins, vocal
Eyelyn "Daisy" Perry, vocal
Pam Perry, mandolin, vocal
Ford Philpot
Eddie Price, vocal
Coy Priddy, mandolin, vocal

Vernon Rainwater, vocal
Howard Rainwater (Crusaders
    Quartet), vocal
Dempsey Rainwater (Crusaders
    Quartet), vocal
Carmella Ramsey, fiddle
Mary Randolph, vocal
Elsie Randolph (The Randolph
    Sisters), vocal
Jane Randolph (The Randolph
    Sisters), vocal
Shelly Rann, vocal
Wade Ray, fiddle, vocal
"Barefoot" Brownie Reynolds,
    bass, vocal
Marge Rhoads (The Rhoads),
    vocal
Debby Rhoads (The Rhoads),
    vocal
Deanie Richardson, fiddle
Bob Roark, vocal
Chris Robbins, vocal
James Roberts, vocal
Lou Ann Roberts, vocal
Jenny Robinson, vocal
Jewell Robinson, vocal
Kaliesa Robinson, clog dancer
Virginia Robinson, vocal
Justin Rogers, clog dancer
Sandy Rudder, vocal

"Harmonica" Bill Russell
Bonnie Runge, vocal
Russell Brothers, bluegrass band
Harold Russell, mandolin, vocal

Jake Salsbury, comedy
Maud Salsbury, comedy
Buster Samples, guitar, vocal
Curly Ray Sanders, vocal
Bernece Scott (The Blue Moun-
    tain Girls), vocal
Steve Sears, vocal
Jim Sexton, vocal
Daisy Sexton, vocal
Juanita Shehan, vocal
Nettie Shehan
Shorty Shehan, fiddle
Steve Shepard, vocal
Dick Shuey, vocal
Bob Simmons, fiddle
Vicki Simmons, bass, vocal
Kit Simunick, harmonica
Tim Sisco, vocal
Gene Sloan, guitar
Bobby Sloan, fiddle
Hal Smith, fiddle
Robyn Smith, vocal
Sandy Smith, vocal
Ray Sosby, fiddle
Tommy Sosby, vocal
Deanna Sowder, vocal
Ernie Sowder, vocal
Darrell Speck, vocal
Doug Spivey, vocal
Al Staas, announcer
Arnold Staley, vocal
Pete Stamper, comedy, vocal,
    emcee
Jeanne Steele, vocal
Mel Steele, vocal
Lou Ann Stegall, vocal
Carrie Stone, vocal
Chick Sullivan, bass, vocal

Marion Sumner, fiddle
Virginia Sutton, vocal
Claud Sweet, vocal

Marvin Tayler, vocal
John J. Teater, emcee
Terre Haute Boys, vocal
Rhuel Thomas, gospel vocal
Flossie Thomas, gospel vocal
Glenn Thompson, guitar
Scott Thompson, drums, vocal
Shane Thompson, vocal
Susan Tomes, guitar, vocal
Miss Patty Towery, organ
Ruby Travis (Travis Twins), vocal
Ruth Travis (Travis Twins), vocal
Gabe Tucker, comedy, trumpet,
    emcee
Lige Turner, vocal
Red Turner, vocal
Wayne Turner, vocal
Curly Tuttle, vocal

Tonya Virgin, vocal

Billy Wagers, drums
Dora May Wagers, banjo
Jim Waggoner, gospel vocal
Wes Waggoner, gospel vocal
Henry "Scrub Board" Wallace,
    comedy
Brenda Wallin, vocal
Smokey Ward, fiddle, emcee
Jeff Watson, vocal
Craig Wells, vocal
Bonnie Whitaker, guitar
Clarence Williams, comedy, vocal
Tom Williams, vocal
Woody Williams, vocal
Charlie Williams, vocal
Bun Wilson, comedy, vocal
Wayne Wilson, vocal
Dave Woollum (Laurel County
    Boys), vocal
Fred Wooten, steel
Jennifer Wrinkle, fiddle

Betty Lou York, comedy

Index

Index